AMERICAN REGIONAL THEATRE HISTORY TO 1900:
A Bibliography

compiled by
Carl F. W. Larson

The Scarecrow Press, Inc.
Metuchen, N.J., & London
1979

PN
2221
L34

Library of Congress Cataloging in Publication Data

Larson, Carl F   W   1939–
    American regional theatre history to 1900.

    Includes indexes.
    1. Theater--United States--Bibliography.
I. Title.
Z5781.L34 [PN2221]   016.792'0973   79-11282
ISBN 0-8108-1216-9

For my parents
Elmer and Elvera Larson
with thanks

CONTENTS

PREFACE

This bibliography attempts to provide access to research on the history of American regional theatre up to
1900, excluding New York City. It lists books, periodical
articles, essays in anthologies, theses, completed dissertations, sections of local history books, newspaper articles
and some manuscript reports which concentrate on the dramatic history of a specified geographic area. Since Clifford
Hamar's pioneering effort in 1949, many additional studies of
local theatre history have been completed, but it has always
been time consuming to locate them because many of them
are masters' theses, which are little publicized, or are periodical articles in regional history journals, which have only
recently been more systematically indexed. In any case, the
material has been widely scattered, and it has been difficult
to get a sense of what work has been done for a specific region. It is hoped that this work will make possible kinds of
research which could not heretofore be pursued.

This volume attempts to cover the entire United States,
state by state, and city by city, listing entries chronologically by date of coverage. This arrangement seemed to be
much more useful than the one used by Carl J. Stratman in
his Bibliography of the American Theatre Excluding New York
City (1965) which lists chronologically by publication date,
thereby intermingling research on previous eras with reports
of current twentieth-century dramatic activities. Clarence
Gohdes' Literature and Theater of the States and Regions of
the USA (1967) does the same thing, using an alphabetical arrangement, and, in addition, does not provide a breakdown
according to individual cities. This work is greatly indebted
to both the Stratman and Gohdes books for information and
inspiration, as well as for the frustration which led to the
current format for presenting references.

This work was begun by gathering relevant citations
from Stratman and Gohdes which were later verified and corrected during the summer of 1977 at the University of South-

vii

ern California and at UCLA. I have personally examined almost all of the periodical articles cited herein and have corrected numerous entries. The two previously cited volumes contained various errors, perhaps because assistants were used and certainly because the indexes used themselves contained errors. By examining the articles, I have been able to cite those such as item 155 that were in fact continuations of previous articles though their titles did not make this clear and those such as 594 where all subsequent relevant issues were not cited. I have moved item 585 from Texas, in Stratman, to Massachusetts and returned 1168 to South Dakota, which Stratman had given to North Dakota. In addition, articles have been deleted, such as one entitled "The Georgetown-Leadville Stage" which dealt with stage coaches. Other corrections involve titles, names and pagination.

Additional entries were gathered from the National Union Catalog, Comprehensive Dissertation Index, 1861-1972, Dissertation Abstracts International, Litto's American Dissertations on the Drama and the Theatre: A Bibliography, Writings on American History, America: History and Life, Speech Monographs, and Bibliographic Annual in Speech Communication, as well as from several other miscellaneous bibliographies published in regional history journals and elsewhere. Some items were gleaned from the bibliographies in some of the other works cited, but no attempt has been made to examine every bibliography in every work listed.

The reference librarians at all schools which held relevant masters' and in some cases bachelors' theses were contacted and asked to verify the citations. Most, but not all, cheerfully responded, and also provided additional references. In addition, the reference librarians at all the remaining schools which offered graduate work in English and/ or drama were asked to submit relevant citations. As a result, numerous additional entries came to light.

I am deeply indebted to the many hundreds of reference librarians who so kindly assisted me in verifying entries and in providing dates of coverage, and in some cases, city coverage as well. Without their help, this work could not be arranged as it now is. Finally, all relevant doctoral dissertations were separately verified by the reference librarians of the schools concerned, and I am equally indebted to their thoroughness and promptness. I thank the many reference librarians, not only for the information they provided, but for the many kind words of encouragement and for the

enthusiastic support for this project which they conveyed to
me as well.

Users should note certain limitations to the present
volume. Reprints of books are not listed, nor are reprints
in book form of periodical material (e.g. item 441). Dissertations announced in the annual Educational Theatre Journal listings are not included unless they later appeared in
Dissertation Abstracts International. Some articles (e.g. 977)
have sequels continuing coverage beyond 1900; such sequels
if devoted to the twentieth century exclusively are not here
listed. The work focuses naturally on English-language theatre; some foreign-language theatre is also included (see index), but it is probably considerably less complete. Although there are some citations to sections of regional history books, no systematic search of most regional history
books has been made.

Two other limitations should also be noted. Periodical
articles published before 1900 are not included, unlike in
Stratman, unless the focus of the article is primarily historical. For the most part, books published before 1900 deal-
ing with the then contemporary scene are also omitted. Because Stratman uses date of publication for his entry order,
most of those books can most readily be found in that book,
especially for Boston and Philadelphia. Second, this work
lists material on actors, actresses and other theatre personnel only if they are tied to a specific geographic area in the
title or through personal verification of the entry. See the
Persons as Subject Index for a key to those citations. Un-
doubtedly, considerable additional material is available on
theatre personnel which is in fact localized to a specific area
although the title does not so indicate--but that material has
not been pursued here. Memoirs of actors and actresses
are also excluded.

Entries for specific cities are arranged chronologically by date of coverage but with some variation between entries on how the dates are determined. Some librarians
have cited the first date mentioned, others the first date of
significance. Users will sometimes need to enlarge their
chronological range to secure some entries. Entries which
have an unknown opening date are placed immediately before
the closing date. Undated items are placed at the end of
the entries for a specific city. Some unverified entries may
in fact cover twentieth-century material only. Some are in-
complete. Several items are entered in more than one place

(with a different entry number). The section labeled General, included for most states, contains those items which are not limited to a single city. Most such entries are broken down by having the cities covered listed alphabetically. The number in brackets at the end of a dissertation entry is the University Microfilm order number, thus showing at a glance which items are available from that source. A few masters' theses are also available on microfilm; their numbers are also indicated. Because locating an item was deemed most important, the names of colleges and universities have been changed to reflect current (1978) usage.

At the end of the state entries, regional categories are listed. The items in those subdivisions are somewhat arbitrarily assigned since what is south to some is east to others, an example of a nationwide complication which makes tidy categories impossible. The East section is rather miscellaneous in that it contains various items more general in scope than does the rest of the book. Many more items could doubtless be included using such criteria. The Miscellaneous section contains items deemed important which did not fit in any other categories. The bibliographies, listed at the end, before the indexes, are to a large degree superseded by the present work. They are listed because they contain additional material on modern drama history, on manuscript sources, or on other useful works. Readers should also note the National List of Historic Theatre Buildings, a very useful pamphlet compiled by Gene Chesley, University of California, Davis.

New York City is excluded from this book, but there are a few citations on it included in other sections, e. g. item 1295. There are several items in the South section on Confederate drama, citations which I thought could very easily be lost.

I have tried to make this work as accurate, complete, and useful as possible. But a work taken up and set aside innumerable times and sandwiched between a nearly full-time teaching load and administrative responsibilities as well is likely to be subject to oversights and inconsistencies. I would very much appreciate receiving corrections and information on additional pertinent citations which users may care to provide for any possible future editions or supplements.

It is a pleasure to thank all those who have assisted with this work in various ways. I wish space considerations

did not preclude listing by name the many hundreds of reference librarians who so graciously assisted me. To them I
am most grateful. Dr. Richard Toscan of the University of
Southern California provided strong encouragement for this
project at an early and crucial stage. Special thanks are
due to Carol Cornell, Roberta Barabash Anderson, Jean
Roszkowski, Sylvia Reisinger and Carolyn Lardy for excellent
typing. But my greatest debt is to my wife, Esther, who not
only has lived with and encouraged this whole project but who
typed much of it during its development and who typed the
entire final manuscript. Without her encouragement and work
this book could not be what it now is. I must also thank our
three-year-old son, Carlton, who last summer kept asking
me if I was doing "hard research." He has had a part in
this as well.

CARL F. W. LARSON
Dickinson State College
Dickinson, North Dakota

ALABAMA

BIRMINGHAM

1 Haarbauer, Don Ward. "A Critical History of the Non-Academic Theatre in Birmingham, Alabama. " Ph. D. University of Wisconsin, Madison, 1973. v, 423 p. [73-20251] (1872-)

2 Chiles, Ruth. "The Birmingham Theatres, 1886-1900. " M. A. Birmingham-Southern College, 1936.

3 O'Brien, Mrs. Frank P. "Birmingham's Early Play Houses. " Early Days in Birmingham. Birmingham: Birmingham Publishing Co. , 1937.

MOBILE

4 Duggar, Mary Morgan. "The Theatre in Mobile, 1822-1860. " M. A. University of Alabama, 1941. 247 p.

5 Walton, Elsie Marie. "A History of Theatre in Mobile, Alabama, 1822-1971. " M. A. Pennsylvania State University, 1971.

6 Bailey, Frances Margaret. "A History of the Stage in Mobile, Alabama, from 1824-1850. " M. A. University of Iowa, 1934. vii, 362 p.

7 Woodruff, Boykin Maxwell, Jr. "A Chronicle of Professional Dramatic Activities at the Mobile Theatre under the Management of Jacob Tannenbaum from 1844 through 1889. " M. A. University of Georgia, 1975.

8 Brown, Edward Devereaux. "A History of Theatrical Activities at the Mobile Theatre, Mobile, Alabama, from 1860-1875. " M. A. Michigan State University, 1952. 183 p.

1

MONTGOMERY

9   Adams, Henry Welch. "The History of the Theatre in
    Montgomery, Alabama, 1815-1835. " M. A. Columbia
    University, 1950.

10 _____ . The Montgomery Theatre, 1822-1835. Uni-
    versity, Alabama, 1955. University of Alabama
    Studies, No. 9. 81 p.

11 Turnipseed, La Margaret. "The Ante-bellum Theatre in
    Montgomery, Alabama: 1840-1860. " M. S. Auburn
    University, 1948. 94 p.

12 O'Brien, Frank P. "Passing of the Old Montgomery
    Theatre. " Alabama Historical Quarterly, 3 (Spring,
    1941), 8-14. (1860-)

GENERAL

13 Gordon, Barbara E. "Prosperous and Preposterous
    Theatres in Alabama, 1817-1860. " M. A. University
    of North Carolina, Chapel Hill, 1971.

14 Nolan, Paul T. "Alabama Drama, 1870-1916: A Check
    List. " Alabama Review, 18 (January, 1965), 65-72.

    See also 1426.

ALASKA

GENERAL

15 Saloutos, Theodore. "Alexander Pantages, Theater Mag-
    nate of the West. " Pacific Northwest Quarterly, 57
    (October, 1966), 137-147. (1898-1936)

ARIZONA

SONORA

16 Gipson, Rosemary. "The Beginning of Theatre in Sono-
      ra." Arizona and the West, 9 (Winter, 1967), 349-
      364. (1850's-1880)

TOMBSTONE

17 Willson, Clair Eugene. "A History of the Theatrical
      Activities of Tombstone, Arizona, from 1880-1918."
      M. S. Northwestern University, 1934.

18 _____. Mimes and Miners: A Historical Study of the
      Theatre in Tombstone. Tucson: University of Ari-
      zona. "University of Arizona Bulletin," Vol. 6, No.
      7 (October 1, 1935). Fine Arts Bulletin, No. 1.
      207 p.

19 _____. "From Variety Theater to Coffee Shoppe."
      Arizona Historical Review, 6 (April, 1935), 3-13.
      (1881-1892)

20 Ryan, Pat M. Tombstone Theatre Tonight: A Chron-
      icle of Entertainment on the Southwestern Mining
      Frontier. Tucson, Arizona, 1966. Smoke Signal,
      No. 13 (Spring, 1966), 51-76.

      See also 1452, 1453.

TUCSON

21 Gipson, Rosemary Pechin. "The Mexican Performers:
      Pioneer Theatre Artists of Tucson." Journal of Ari-
      zona History, 13 (Winter, 1972), 235-252. (1850's-
      1880's)

22 _____. "The History of Tucson Theatre before 1906."
      M. A. University of Arizona, 1967. 203 p. (1870's-)

      See also 1452.

ARKANSAS

DARDANELLE

See 31.

FAYETTEVILLE

23 Finsel, Tamara Jeanne Valley. "The History of the Theatre at the University of Arkansas from 1893 to the Summer of 1973. " M. A. University of Arkansas, 1974.

See also 31.

FORT GIBSON

See 30.

FORT SMITH

See 31.

LITTLE ROCK

24 Wooten, Denham Lee. "Annals of the Stage in Little Rock, Arkansas, 1834-1890. " M. A. Columbia University, 1935. 159 p.

25 Stokes, D. Allen. "The First Theatrical Season in Arkansas: Little Rock, 1838-1839. " Arkansas Historical Quarterly, 23 (Summer, 1964), 166-183.

26 Reed, Charles E. , Jr. "An Historical Study of Professional Dramatic Entertainment in Little Rock, Arkansas, 1889-1899. " M. A. University of Florida, 1949.

27 Menefee, Larry Thomas. "Death of a Road Show Town: Little Rock, Arkansas, 1899-1921. " Ph. D. University of Denver, 1977. 354 p. [77-22778]

See also 30.

RUSSELLVILLE

See 31.

TEXARKANA

28 Clark, Linda Kidd. "A Theater History of Texarkana
       from 1876 through 1924. " M. S. East Texas State Uni-
       versity, 1972.

VAN BUREN

See 31.

GENERAL

29 Moffatt, Walter. "Cultural and Recreational Activities in
       Pioneer Arkansas. " Arkansas Historical Quarterly,
       13 (Winter, 1954), 372-385. (1820-1839)

30 _____. "First Theatrical Activities in Arkansas. "
       Arkansas Historical Quarterly, 12 (Winter, 1953),
       327-332. (Fort Gibson, Little Rock) (1834-1839)

31 Tedford, Harold Calvin. "A Study of the Theatrical
       Entertainments in Northwest Arkansas from Their
       Beginnings through 1889. " Ph. D. Louisiana State Uni-
       versity, 1965. 342 p. [66-00750] (Dardanelle, Fay-
       etteville, Fort Smith, Russellville, Van Buren) (1838-)

32 Nolan, Paul T. , and Amos E. Simpson. "Arkansas
       Drama before World War I: An Unexplored Country. "
       Arkansas Historical Quarterly, 22 (Spring, 1963),
       61-75. (1865-1916)

33 Hunter, John Marvin, Sr. "Mollie Bailey, Great Show-
       woman. " Frontier Times, 27 (April, 1950), 183-193.
       (1866-1918)

34 Wooten, Denham. "The History of the Theatre in Ark-
       ansas. " Arkansas Gazette, mag. sec. , November 17
       and 24, December 9, 15, and 22, 1935.

See also 1421.

CALIFORNIA

AUBURN

35 Perry, May W. "Auburn's Opera House. " Placer Nuggets, February, 1959, pp. 1-7.

COLUMBIA

36 Broadbent, Thomas L. "The Schiller Centennial in Columbia: California Germans in a Gold Rush Town. " American German Review, 29 (August-September, 1963), 7-13. (1859-)

See also 118.

EUREKA

37 Bettendorf, Frank Bernard. "Dramatic Activities of the Humboldt Bay Area 1880 to 1912. " M. A. University of California, Los Angeles, 1963.

FRESNO

38 Walker, Phillip Nathaniel. "A History of Theatrical Activity in Fresno, California, from Its Beginnings in 1872 to the Opening of the White Theatre in 1914. " Ph. D. University of Southern California, 1972. 2 vols. 579 p. [73-00786]

39 Smith, Larry A. "The History of the Barton Opera House, Fresno, California: 1890-1914. " M. A. California State University, Fresno, 1970.

GRASS VALLEY

See 123.

LOS ANGELES

40 Tyler, Pamela F. "The Los Angeles Theatre, 1840-1900. " M. A. University of Southern California, 1942.

41 Barnett, Martha Ione. "A Historical Sketch of the Professional Theatre in the City of Los Angeles to 1911. " M. A. University of Southern California, 1930.

42 Yaari, Moshe. "The Merced Theatre. " Historical Society of Southern California Quarterly, 37 (September, 1955), 195-210. (1870-1955)

43 Kaufman, Edward Kenneth. "A History of the Development of Professional Theatrical Activity in Los Angeles, 1880-1895. " Ph. D. University of Southern California, 1972. 419 p. [73-07254]

44 Woods, Alan Lambert. "The Interaction of Los Angeles Theater and Society Between 1895 and 1906: A Case Study. " Ph. D. University of Southern California, 1972. 2 vols. 521 p. [73-00792]

45 _____. "Popular Theater in Los Angeles at the Turn of the Century. " Players, 48 (April-May, 1973), 173-178. (1896, 1898)

46 Robinson, Giles Frederick. "A Historical Study of Dramatic Activities at the University of Southern California. " M. A. University of Southern California, 1957. 107 p.

See also 117, 118.

MARYSVILLE

See 79, 123, 1453.

MONTEREY

47 Andresen, Anna G. "California's First Theater, at Monterey. (State Aid for Its Restoration). " Grizzly Bear, 20 (January, 1917), 5.

48 Scheff, Aimee. "California's First Theatre. " Theatre Arts, 37 (May, 1953), 78. (1848)

49 Hume, Robert Douglas. "California's First Theatre. " Carolina Play-Book, 16 (December, 1943), 131-134.

50 Peters, Rollo. "Horse Opera House. " Theatre Arts, 28 (February, 1944), 117-122. (1875-)

See also 115, 118, 119.

NEVADA CITY

51 Stewart, George R. , Jr.   "The Drama in a Frontier
    Theatre. " The Parrott Presentation Volume.   Ed.
    Hardin Craig.   Princeton, N. J. :   Princeton University
    Press, 1935.   pp. 183-204.   (1856-1858)

See also 79, 118.

OAKLAND

52 Wente, William Charles.   "The Oakland Theatre, 1890-
    1915. "   Ph. D. Stanford University, 1965.   v, 393 p.
    [65-12885]

OROVILLE

See 79, 123.

PASADENA

See 117.

PLACERVILLE

See 123.

RIVERSIDE

53 Conn, Arthur Leslie.   "The History of the Loring Opera
    House, Riverside, California. " M. A. University of
    California, Los Angeles, 1970.   (1890-)

54 Freud, Ralph.   "Frank A. Miller: Theater Manager. "
    Historical Society of Southern California Quarterly,
    41 (March, 1959), 5-10.   (1890)

SACRAMENTO

55 Hume, Charles Vernard.   "The Sacramento Theatre,
    1849-1885. "   Ph. D. Stanford University, 1955.   v,
    499 p.   [00-12268]

56 _____ .   "First of the Gold Rush Theatres. " Cali-
    fornia Historical Society Quarterly, 46 (December,
    1967), 337-344.   (1849)

57 The Beginnings of Drama in Sacramento, 1849 and 1949.
    Compiled and written by students of C. K. McClatchy
    Senior High School.   Sacramento: Nugget Press,
    1955.   25 p.

58 McGowan, Joseph A.   History of the Sacramento Valley.
    New York: Lewis Historical Publishing Co. , 1961.
    Vol. 1, pp. 141-147; Vol. 2, pp. 153-156.

59 McClatchy, Charles K.   ". . . Recollections of the Drama
    of Days Gone By. "   Sacramento Bee, Sept. 27, 1924,
    p. L-3.

    See also 79, 118, 119, 123, 1453.

SAN BERNARDINO

    See 117.

SAN DIEGO

60 Lane, Morgan J.   "Commercial Theatre in San Diego
    with Special Emphasis 1892-1917. "   M. A. San Diego
    State University, 1969.

    See also 115, 117.

SAN FRANCISCO

61 Ker, Minette Augusta.   "The History of the Theatre in
    California in the Nineteenth Century. "   M. A. Uni-
    versity of California, Berkeley, 1924.   (1830?-1900)

62 Egan, Frank.   "Minstrelsy in San Francisco: 1848-1870. "
    M. A. California State University, Sacramento, 1971.

63 Sawyer, Eugene T.   "Hamlets I Have Seen and Other
    Hamlets: Early Theatrical Days in San Francisco. "
    Overland Monthly, 81 (July, 1923), 13-14, 36-38,
    45-46, 48.   (1840's-)

64 Fenton, Frank L.   "The San Francisco Theatre, 1849-
    1859. "   Ph. D. Stanford University, 1942.   iv, 428 p.

65 Webster, Mary Viola.   "The San Francisco Stage: A
    Daily Calendar of Performances, 1849-1859. "   M. A.
    California State University, Northridge, 1974.   146 p.

66 Demarest, Michael. "Music to Which the Gold Rushed. "
    Opera and Concert, 15 (1950), 9-11; 15 (1950), 15-16.
    (1849-1902)

67 Gaer, Joseph, ed. The Theatre of the Gold Rush Decade
    in San Francisco. California Literary Research
    Project, Monograph 5. 1935. 99 p. (1850-1859)

68 Estavan, Lawrence, ed. San Francisco Theatre Re-
    search ... Monographs. San Francisco, 1938-1942.
    20 vols.

69 Chester, Violet Lercara. "The History of the Theatre
    in San Francisco from the Gold Rush to the Con-
    flagration of 1906. " M. A. Stanford University, 1930.

70 McCurdy, Evelyn Mary. "The History of the Adelphi
    Theatre, San Francisco, California, 1850-1858. "
    M. A. Stanford University, 1952. 96 p.

71 Benoff, Stephen Michael. "The Jenny Lind Theatre. "
    M. A. University of California, Los Angeles, 1966.
    (1850-1852)

72 Harrington, Donal F. "Productions of Shakespeare in
    San Francisco from 1850 through 1855. " M. A.
    Columbia University, 1933.

73 Mering, Yolla. "The San Francisco Theatrical Career
    of Dr. D. G. Robinson. " M. A. California State Uni-
    versity, Long Beach, 1977. 166 p. (1850-1856)

74 Rodecape, Lois Foster. "Tom Maguire, Napoleon of the
    Stage. " California Historical Society Quarterly, 20
    (December, 1941), 289-314; 21 (March, 1942), 39-74;
    (June, 1942), 141-182; (September, 1942), 239-275.
    (1850-)

75 Whitehead, Marjorie. "Sarah Kirby Stark: California's
    Pioneer Actress-Manager. " M. A. California State
    University, Sacramento, 1972. (1850-)

76 Rea, J. "Seeing the Elephant. " Western Folklore, 28
    (January, 1969), 21-26. (1850)

77 Fenton, Frank L. "Old San Francisco: Hatchery of
    Theater. " Asides: ... An Informal Publication, No.
    2 (1941), pp. 1-16. (1850-1860)

78 Hughes, Myrna B. "Questionnaires on Drama in Old
    San Francisco." Asides: ... An Informal Publi-
    cation, No. 2, (1941), pp. i-viii.

79 Holmes, Susan Carol. "Junius Brutus Booth, Jr.: A
    Pioneer Actor-Manager of the California Stage."
    M. A. San Jose State University, 1971. (Marysville,
    Nevada City, Oroville, Sacramento, Stockton, Virginia
    City) (1851-1864)

80 Gagey, Edmond McAdoo. The San Francisco Stage, A
    History: Based on Annals Compiled by the Research
    Department of the San Francisco Federal Theatre.
    New York: Columbia University Press, 1950. 264 p.
    (1852-1899)

81 Rogers, Virginia Marion. "Caroline Chapman, American
    Actress; Her Contributions to the San Francisco
    Stage." M. A. Stanford University, 1940. (1852-)

82 Madison, James. "Some Shadows of the San Francisco
    Stage." California Historical Society Quarterly, 4
    (March, 1925), 59-63. (1852-)

83 _____. "Early San Francisco Theatres." Collector's
    Guide, No. 24 (December, 1940), 3-6. (See also the
    issues for January to March, 1939)

84 Shattuck, Charles H. "Edwin Booth's First Critic."
    Theatre Survey, 7 (May, 1966), 1-14. (1852-1855)

85 Avedisian, Louise Joanne. "Lola Montez in California
    (1853-1856)." M. A. University of California, Los
    Angeles, 1971.

86 Von Ostwalden, Claudia Weber. "The Beginnings of
    German Theater in San Francisco." M. A. University
    of California, Davis, 1973. 79 p. (1853-1862)

87 McCabe, John Herbert. "Historical Essay on the Drama
    in California." First Annual Report of the Territorial
    Pioneers of California, 1877, pp. 72-78.

88 Gates, Harry. "Early Theatricals on the Pacific Coast."
    San Francisco Call, mag. sec., March 17, 24, 31,
    April 21, 28, June 16, 23, 1901.

89 Jacobson, Pauline. "California's First Playhouses. "
    San Francisco Bulletin, August 19, 26, September 2,
    1916.

90 (French theaters of pioneer days). San Francisco Chron-
    icle, November 16, 1950, mag. sec. , p. 8.

91 Galloway, R. Dean. "Rowena Granice; or, Mistress of
    Her Fate. " Unpublished manuscript (1970), 28 p.
    (1856-1859)

92 Wade, Jere Dueffort. "The San Francisco Stage, 1859-
    1869. " Ph. D. University of Oregon, 1972. iv, 220 p.
    [72-20934]

93 Loomis, Charles Grant. "The German Theater in San
    Francisco, 1861-1864. " University of California Pub-
    lications in Modern Philology, Vol. 36, No. 8 (1952),
    193-242.

94 Sawyer, Eugene T. "Old-Time Minstrels of San Fran-
    cisco ... Recollections of a Pioneer. " Overland
    Monthly, 81 (October, 1923), 5-7. (1860's)

95 _____. "Old Players of San Francisco. " Overland
    Monthly, 82 (February, 1924), 59, 76-77, 79.
    (1860's-)

96 Krumm, Walter Courtney. "The San Francisco Stage,
    1869-1879. " Ph. D. Stanford University, 1961. viii,
    206 p. [61-04143]

97 Robertson, Peter. "Great Actors of Old San Francisco. "
    Pacific Monthly, 19 (May, 1908), 494-505; 20 (July,
    1908), 2-14; (October, 1908), 434-444; (November,
    1908), 527-538. (1869-)

98 Griffiths, Philip Ray. "A History of the Emerson Min-
    strels on the San Francisco Stage, 1870-1889. " M. A.
    Stanford University, 1954. 142 p.

99 Alexander, Doris M. "The Passion Play in America. "
    American Quarterly, 11 (Fall, 1959), 351-371.
    (1879-)

100 McElhaney, John Scott. "The Professional Theater in
    San Francisco: 1880-1889. " Ph. D. Stanford Uni-
    versity, 1972. vii, 386 p. [72-30667]

101 Kadelburg, Heinrich. Fünfzehn Jahre des deutschen Theaters in San Francisco: Ein Ruckblick, nebst Personal--und Repertoire--verzeichniss. San Francisco: Druck von Rosenthal und Roesch, 1883. 32 p.

102 Hall, Linda. "Lillie Langtry and the American West." Journal of Popular Culture, 7 (Spring, 1974), 873-881. (1880's)

103 Poultney, George W. "Famous American Theatres." Theatre Arts, 42 (September, 1958), 56. (1888-)

104 Staples, Frank. "History of the Theatre in San Francisco." Overland Monthly, 85 (January, 1927), 17, 22-23, 25. (1890's)

See also 118, 119, 123, 1452, 1453.

SAN JOAQUIN VALLEY

105 Larimer, Michael W. "Theatre in the San Joaquin Valley: A Pilot Study of Theatrical Activities, 1870-1900." M.A. California State University, Fresno, 1969.

SAN JOSE

106 Sawyer, Eugene. History of Santa Clara County California. Los Angeles: Historic Record Co., 1922. Chapter 9, pp. 118-125. (1859-)

SANTA BARBARA

107 Smith, Tallant. "The History of the Theatre in Santa Barbara: 1769-1894." M.A. University of California, Santa Barbara, 1969. 191 p.

SANTA CLARA

108 Spearman, A.D. "California's First Stage." Academy Scrapbook, 1 (April, 1951), 289-292. (1794-1830)

SONOMA

109 Curtis, William Albert. "The First Theatre in California." Out West, 28 (June, 1908), 479-482. (1847)

See also 115.

STANFORD

110 Brazee, Annie Laurie. "A History of the Theatre at Stanford University (1891-1906). " M. A. Stanford University, 1952. 208 p.

STOCKTON

111 Noid, Benjamin Maynard. "History of the Theatre in Stockton, California, 1850-1892. " Ph. D. University of Utah, 1968. 2 vols. xvi, 562 p. [69-03490]

112 _____. "Stockton Theater: The Lost Nugget. " Pacific Historian, 13 (Summer, 1969), 15-25. (1850's-)

See also 79, 118, 123.

VISALIA

113 Monson, William Neil. "Frontier Theatre Town: An Historical Study of Some Paratheatrical Activities in Visalia, California, 1852 to 1889. " Ph. D. University of Oregon, 1976. 2 vols. viii, 398 p. [77-13206]

WOODLAND

114 McDermott, Douglas, and Robert K. Sarlos. "The Woodland 'Hershey' Opera House: The End of an Era in California Theatre. " California Historical Society Quarterly, 48 (December, 1969), 291-306. (1896-1913)

See also 118.

GENERAL

115 Allison, Tempe E. "The Theater in Early California. " University of California Chronicle, 30 (January, 1928), 75-79. (Monterey, San Diego, Sonoma) (1832, 1846-1847)

116 MacMinn, George Rupert. The Theater of the Golden Era in California. Caldwell, Idaho: The Caxton Printers, Ltd. , 1941. 529 p. (1846-1860)

15 California

117 Earnest, Sue Wolfer. "An Historical Study of the
    Growth of the Theatre in Southern California, 1848-
    1894. " Ph. D. University of Southern California,
    1947. 3 vols. 1,063 p. (Los Angeles, Pasadena,
    San Bernardino, San Diego, etc.)

118 Early Theatres of California. San Francisco: Book
    Club of California, 1974, 11 folders. (Columbia,
    Los Angeles, Monterey, Nevada City, Sacramento,
    San Francisco, Stockton, Woodland)

119 Allison, Tempe. "Memories Theatrical. " Theatre and
    School, 9 (May, 1931), 3-7. (Monterey, Sacramento,
    San Francisco) (1843, 1849, 1853)

120 McCabe, John H. "The Drama in California in '49 and
    '50. " Grissly Bear, 26 (March, 1920), 3.

121 McDermott, Douglas. "Touring Patterns on California's
    Theatrical Frontier, 1849-1859. " Theatre Survey,
    15 (May, 1974), 18-28.

122 Rodecape, Lois. "Celestial Drama in the Golden Hills:
    The Chinese Theatre in California, 1849-1869. "
    California Historical Society Quarterly, 23 (June,
    1944), 97-116.

123 Clarke, Shareen Merriam. "The Child Stars of the
    Far West: 1849-1865. " M. A. San Jose State Uni-
    versity, 1971. (Grass Valley, Marysville, Oroville,
    Placerville, Sacramento, San Francisco, Stockton,
    Virginia City)

124 Ausburn, Lynna Joyce. "Highlights of the Theatre of
    the West: Its Beginnings and Its Development on the
    Mining Frontiers of California and Nevada. " M. A.
    University of Tulsa, 1970. 148 p. (1849-1860's)

125 McCloskey, J. J. "Lizzy Bingham, the First California
    Actress. " San Jose Pioneer, 14 (1899), 147-148.

126 Trulsson, Berton E. "A Historical Study of the Theatre
    of the Mother Lode During the Gold Rush Period. " M. A.
    University of the Pacific, 1950. 133 p. (1851-1861)

127 Hume, Charles V. "The Gold Rush Actor: His For-
    tunes and Misfortunes in the Mining Camps. " Ameri-
    can West, 9 (May, 1972), 14-19. (1850's)

128   Brereton, Roslyn. "The Glamorous Gold Rush: Great
       Stage Stars in California and Victoria in the 1850's. "
       Pacific Historian, 13 (Summer, 1969), 6-14.

129   Dorst, Kenneth Robert. "A Descriptive Investigation of
       the Theatrical Structures Built by Thomas Maguire
       in the Far West. " Ph. D. University of Denver,
       1966. 226 p. [67-03941] (1854-1896)

130   McCloskey, J. J. "The Drama in Old California. "
       Green Room Album, March, 1911, pp. 655-660.

131   Fenton, Frank L. , ed. Pioneer Western Playbills.
       San Francisco, 1951.

132   McKee, Irving. "Artemus Ward in California and Ne-
       vada, 1863-1864. " Pacific Historical Review, 20
       (February, 1951), 11-24.

133   Ryan, Patrick M. , Jr. "Mark Twain: Frontier Theatre
       Critic. " Arizona Quarterly, 16 (Summer, 1960),
       197-208. (1863-1866)

134   Krythe, Maymie Richardson. "Madame Modjeska in
       California. " The Historical Society of Southern
       California Quarterly, 35 (March, 1953), 29-40.
       (1875-1909)

135   Goss, Helen Rocca. "Lillie Langtry and Her California
       Ranch. " Historical Society of Southern California
       Quarterly, 37 (June, 1955), 161-176.

       See also 1451, 1454, 1472.

COLORADO

ASPEN

136   Riker, Kittie Blanchard. "Theatrical Activity in Aspen,
       Colorado, from 1881 to 1893. " M. A. University of
       Colorado, 1964.

137 Shaw, Bertha Louise. "History of the Wheeler Opera,
     Aspen, Colorado, 1889-1894. " M. A. Western State
     College of Colorado, Gunnison, 1965.

CENTRAL CITY

138 Gern, Jesse William. "Colorado Mountain Theatre:
     History of Theatre at Central City, 1859-1885. "
     Ph. D. Ohio State University, 1960. 2 vols. xi,
     626 p. [60-04086]

139 Perrigo, Lynn Irwin. "A Social History of Central
     City, Colorado, 1859-1900. " Ph. D. University of
     Colorado, 1936. pp. 296-311, 496-511.

140 _____. "The First Two Decades of Central City
     Theatricals. " Colorado Magazine, 11 (July, 1934),
     141-152. (1860-1880)

141 Sayre, Hal. "Early Central City Theatricals and Other
     Reminiscences. " Colorado Magazine, 6 (March,
     1929), 47-53. (1860-)

142 Bayly, Charles, Jr. "Opera House at Central City. "
     Theatre Arts Magazine, 16 (March, 1932), 204-213.
     (1878-)

143 _____. The Glory That Was Gold: The Central City
     Opera House. Denver: University of Denver Press,
     1932. 72 p.

144 "Stage: History Reviewed Where Grant Once Walked on
     Silver. " Newsweek, 6 (July 13, 1935), 21-22.
     (1878-)

145 Chapman, John. "The Well-Heeled Ghost, or, There's
     Gold in Them Thar' Arts in Central City. " Theatre
     Arts, 36 (June, 1952), 34-36, 89.

     See also 1453.

CHERRY CREEK

146 Jensen, Billie Barnes. "Entertainment of the 'Fifty-
     Niners. ' " Journal of the West, 5 (January, 1966),
     82-90. (1859)

COLORADO SPRINGS

147 Barnes, Jack Duane. "Simeon Nash Nye, Pioneer Co-
     lorado Theatre Manager, 1882-1914. " Ph. D. Uni-
     versity of Denver, 1972. 373 p. [72-21555] (1873-
     1914)

     See also 1453.

CRAIG

148 Kimball, Neil W. "George M. Kimball--Actor, Editor,
     Pioneer. " Colorado Magazine, 27 (April, 1950),
     89-95. (1890-1930)

CRIPPLE CREEK

149 Adams, Allen John. "A Historical Study of the Legiti-
     mate Theatre in Cripple Creek, Colorado, 1897-1907. "
     M. A. Northern Illinois University, 1967.

150 Donegan, Billie Diane. "An Historical Analysis of
     Theatre Audiences in Cripple Creek, Colorado, from
     1897-1907. " M. A. Colorado State University, 1972.

DENVER

151 Nichols, Dean G. "Pioneer Theatres of Denver, Co-
     lorado. " Ph. D. University of Michigan, 1938.   iv,
     652 p. (1859-1881)

152 Griffin, Evelyn. "Early Theatres and Theatrical Events
     in Denver. " M. A. University of Denver, 1923.
     (1859-1900)

153 Hollingsworth, Mary C. "A History of the Theatre of
     Denver, Colorado. " M. A. University of Southern
     California, 1933. (1859-1932)

154 De la Torre, Lillian. "The Theatre Comes to Denver. "
     Colorado Magazine, 37 (October, 1960), 285-296.
     (1859)

155 _____. "The Haydee Star Company. " Colorado Mag-
     azine, 38 (July, 1961), 201-213. (1859)

156 McConnell, Virginia. "A Gauge of Popular Taste in
      Early Colorado. " Colorado Magazine, 46 (Fall,
      1969), 338-350. (1859-1879)

157 Bell, William Campton. "A History of the Denver
      Theatre During the Post-Pioneer Period (1881-1901). "
      Ph. D. Northwestern University, 1941. 606 p.

158 Crowley, Elmer S. "History of the Tabor Grand Opera
      House, Denver, Colorado, 1881-1891. " M. A. Uni-
      versity of Denver, 1940.

159 _____. "The Opening of the Tabor Grand Opera
      House 1881. " Colorado Magazine, 18 (March, 1941),
      41-48.

160 _____. "An Historic Playhouse Is Born. " Western
      Speech, 10 (March, 1946), 3-7.

161 Kinney, Grover. "Famous American Theatres. " The-
      atre Arts, 40 (December, 1956), 64. (1881-)

162 Parsons, Eugene. "Tabor and His Times. " Trail, 14
      (October, 1921), 3-9. (1881-)

163 Thom, William B. "Stage Celebrities in Denver The-
      atres Forty Years Ago. " Trail, 19 (April, 1927),
      8-13; (May, 1927), 8-14. (1880's-)

164 Zern, Frank W. "Early Day Show Houses and Actors. "
      Trail, 3 (October, 1910), 17-18.

165 Steinhardt, Gertrude Margaret. "Dramatic Episodes in
      the History of the Denver Tabor Grand Opera House. "
      M. A. University of Denver, 1941. (1884-1890)

166 Levy, Edwin Lewis. "Elitch's Gardens, Denver, Co-
      lorado: A History of the Oldest Summer Theatre in
      the United States (1890-1941). " Ph. D. Teachers
      College, Columbia, 1960. 460 p. [60-05831]

      See also 183, 1452, 1453.

GEORGETOWN

167 Klaiber, Roger Charles. "A Historical Study of Theatre
      in Georgetown, Colorado, 1867-1892. " M. A. Uni-
      versity of Colorado, 1964.

GOLDEN

168 Kimball, Neil W. "George M. Kimball--Actor, Editor,
     Pioneer. " Colorado Magazine, 27 (April, 1950),
     89-95. (1890-1930)

GREELEY

169 Jones, Kenneth Lee. "The Theatrical History of Gree-
     ley, Colorado, 1870-1908. " Ph. D. University of
     Denver, 1967. 605 p. [67-17107]

GUNNISON

170 Hatcher, E. Martin. "A History of the Theatre in
     Gunnison, Colorado, and Salida, Colorado, 1880-
     1901. " Ph. D. University of Denver, 1969. 469 p.
     [70-05731]

LEADVILLE

171 Hensley, Michael. "A History of the Theatre in Lead-
     ville, Colorado, from Its Beginning to 1900. " M. A.
     University of Wyoming, 1963.

172 Davis, Ronald L. "They Played for Gold: Theater on
     the Mining Frontier. " Southwest Review, 51 (Spring,
     1966), 169-184. (1870's)

173 Degitz, Dorothy M. "History of the Tabor Opera House,
     Leadville, Colorado, from 1879 to 1905. " M. A.
     Western State College of Colorado, Gunnison, 1935.

174 _____. "History of the Tabor Opera House at Lead-
     ville. " Colorado Magazine, 13 (May, 1936), 81-89.
     (1879-)

175 Griswold, Don L. , and Jean H. Griswold. The Car-
     bonate Camp Called Leadville. Denver: University
     of Denver Press, 1951. pp. 269-275.

     See also 1453.

SALIDA

176 Hatcher, E. Martin. "A History of the Theatre in
     Gunnison, Colorado, and Salida, Colorado, 1880-

1901. " Ph. D. University of Denver, 1969.   469 p.
[70-05731]

GENERAL

177   Davidson, Levette J.   "Shakespeare in the Rockies. "
      Shakespeare Quarterly, 4 (January, 1953), 39-49.
      (1850-1950)

178   Burt, Eliza Logan.   "Recollections of the Early The-
      atre. " Colorado Magazine, 17 (September, 1940),
      161-167. (1850's-)

179   Schoberlin, Melvin H.   "From Candles to Footlights:
      A Chronicle of the Territorial Theater of Colorado:
      A Biography of the Pike's Peak Theatre, 1859-1876. "
      M. A. University of Northern Colorado, 1939.

180   _____. From Candles to Footlights: A Biography
      of the Pike's Peak Theatre, 1859-1876. Denver:
      F. A. Rosenstock, The Old West Publishing Co. ,
      1941. 322 p.

181   Draper, Benjamin Poff.   "Colorado Theatres, 1859-
      1969. " Ph. D. University of Denver, 1969.   5 vols.
      2,127 p. [70-09798]

182   Cochran, Alice.   "Jack Langrishe and the Theater of
      the Mining Frontier. " Colorado Magazine, 46
      (Fall, 1969), 324-337. (1860's-1880's)

183   Adams, Allen John.   "Peter McCourt, Jr. and the
      Silver Theatrical Circuit, 1889-1910: An Historical
      and Biographical Study. " Ph. D. University of
      Utah, 1969.   276 p. [70-02020]

      See also 1451, 1456, 1472.

CONNECTICUT

HARTFORD

184   Burnim, Kalman A.   "Hartford's First Theatre: A
      Chapter in the History of the Old American Com-
      pany. "   Theatre Survey, 9 (November, 1968), 88-
      112.   (1778-1800)

185   "Hartford's New Theatre in 1795. "   Connecticut Quart-
      erly, 2 (April, May, June, 1896), 183.

186   Trumbull, James Hammond.   The Memorial History of
      Hartford County, Connecticut, 1633-1884.   Boston:
      E. L. Osgood, 1886.   Vol. 1, pp. 580-585.

187   Widem, Allen M.   "Famous American Theatres. "
      Theatre Arts, 41 (June, 1957), 81.   (1896-)

188   Parsons' Theatre, Hartford: Twentieth Anniversary
      Historical Souvenir.   April First, Nineteen Sixteen.
      Hartford: The Pyne Printing Co. , 1916?   48 p.

NEW HAVEN

189   Bloom, Arthur William.   "The History of the Theatre
      in New Haven, Connecticut, before 1860. "   Ph. D.
      Yale University, 1966.   437 p.   [66-14942]   (1755-)

190   Thomas, Ota.   "Student Dramatic Activities at Yale
      College During the Eighteenth Century. "   Theatre
      Annual, 3 (1944), 47-59.   (1756-1791)

ROCKVILLE

191   Gourd, E. William.   "A Study of the Henry Opera
      House, Rockville, Connecticut. "   M. F. A.   Ohio Uni-
      versity, 1964.   (1880-1897)

WATERBURY

192   Anderson, Joseph.   "The Drama and Other Amusements. "
      The Town and City of Waterbury, Connecticut, from
      the Aboriginal Period to the Year Eighteen Hundred

and Ninety-Five. New Haven, Conn: The Price &
Lee Co., 1896. Vol. 3, pp. 1091-1117.

GENERAL

See 1408, 1472.

DELAWARE

WILMINGTON

193 Neeson, Jack H. "The Devil in Delaware: A Study of
Theatre in New Castle County. " Ph. D. Case Western
Reserve University, 1959. 2 vols. vii, 626 p.
(1774-1900)

194 _____. "From Schoolhouse to Playhouse: Wilmington's Non-Professional Theatre, 1797-1872. " Delaware History, 8 (March, 1959), 265-293.

195 Conner, William H. "The Life and Death of Wilmington's First Theatre. " Delaware History, 5 (March,
1952), 3-41. (1827-1837)

196 Neeson, Jack, and Margaret Neeson. "Favorite Wilmington Plays before the Civil War. " Delaware
History, 7 (March, 1957), 262-280. (1827-1861)

197 Chance, Elbert. "The Great Days of Wilmington's
Grand Opera House. " Delaware History, 8 (September, 1958), 185-199. (1871-1910)

198 Bond, Roger B. "Wilmington's Masonic Temple and
Grand Opera House. " M. A. University of Delaware,
1969. (1872-1874)

199 Every Evening: History of Delaware. Wilmington, Del.,
1894. pp. 171-173.

200 "Early History of the Drama in Wilmington. " Wilmington Every Evening, April 13, 1895.

201   "Peeping into Wilmington's Departed Theatrical Glories. "
      Wilmington Evening Star, October 29, 1933, mag.
      sec. , pp. 6-7.

202   "Activities of Early Theatre Managers. " Wilmington
      Journal Every Evening, February 14, 1948.

GENERAL

203   Chance, Thomas Elbert.   "A History of Theatre in
      Delaware. " B. A. University of Delaware, 1952.
      245 p.   (1700-)

204   _____.   "History of Delaware Theatre. " Dateline
      Delaware, 2 (January-February, 1961), 23-25;
      (March-April, 1961), 26-28; (May, 1961), 23-25;
      (June, 1961), 29-31.

205   Scharf, John Thomas.   History of Delaware: 1609-1888.
      Philadelphia: L. J. Richards & Co. , 1888.   Vol. 2,
      pp. 793-840.

206   Conrad, Henry Clay.   History of the State of Delaware.
      Wilmington, Del. , 1908.   Vol. 2, pp. 424-426.

DISTRICT OF COLUMBIA

---

207   Kennedy, Mary Augusta.   "The Theatre Movement in
      Washington, 1800-1835. " M. A. Catholic University
      of America, 1933.   46 p.

208   Mudd, Aloysius I.   "Early Theatres in Washington
      City. " Columbia Historical Society Records, 5 (1902),
      64-86.   (1800-1836)

209   _____.   "The Theatres of Washington from 1835-
      1850. " Columbia Historical Society Records, 6 (1903),
      222-266.

210   Coe, Richard L.   "Famous American Theatres. " The-
      atre Arts, 41 (February, 1957), 77, 96.   (1835-)

211 Hunter, Alexander, and Joseph H. Polkinhorn. The New
    National Theater, Washington, D.C., A Record of
    Fifty Years. Washington: R.O. Polkinhorn and
    Son, 1885. 101 p. (1835-1885)

212 Meersman, Roger, and Robert Boyer. "The National
    Theatre in Washington: Buildings and Audiences,
    1835-1972." Records of the Columbia Historical
    Society of Washington, D.C. 1971-1972, 47 (1973),
    190-242.

213 Bloomfield, Maxwell. "Wartime Drama: The Theater
    in Washington (1861-1865)." Maryland Historical
    Magazine, 64 (Winter, 1969), 396-411.

214 Leale, Charles A. "Lincoln's Last Hours." Harper's
    Weekly, 53 (February 13, 1909), 7-10, 27. (1865)

215 Mosby, John S. Jr. "The Night That Lincoln Was
    Shot." Theatre, 17 (June, 1913), 179-180, ix.

216 Sollers, John Ford. "John T. Ford's Theatre." Nat-
    ional Theatre Conference Bulletin, 9 (April, 1947),
    20-26. (1865)

217 Tanner, Cpl. James. "The American Theatre's Most
    Tragic Night. A Factual Account of Lincoln's
    Death." Impresario, February-March, 1962, pp.
    21-23.

218 Tyler, Frederick S. "The Gilbert and Sullivan Operas
    in Washington." Records of the Columbia Historical
    Society, 50 (1948-1950), 71-80. (1896-)

FLORIDA

APALACHICOLA

    See 229.

JACKSONVILLE

219 Parramore, Annie Elaine. "An Historical Study of Theatrical Presentations at the Jacksonville (Florida) Opera House: 1883-1887. " M. A. University of Florida, 1954.

MIAMI

220 Leary, Lewis. "First Theatrical Performance in North America. " American Notes & Queries, 2 (September, 1942), 84. (1567)

221 Cohen, Isidor. Historical Sketches and Sidelights of Miami, Florida. Miami, 1925. Chapter 13.

PENSACOLA

222 Shelley, Dian Lee. "Tivoli Theatre of Pensacola. " Florida Historical Quarterly, 50 (April, 1972), 341-351. (1821-1841)

223 Bagley, Russell Elmer. "An Historical Study of Theatrical Entertainment in Pensacola, Florida, 1882-1892. " M. A. University of Florida, 1949.

224 _____. "Theatrical Entertainment in Pensacola, Florida: 1882-1892. " Southern Speech Journal, 16 (September, 1950), 62-84.

See also 229.

ST. AUGUSTINE

225 Tanner, Helen Hornbeck. "The 1789 Saint Augustine Celebration. " Florida Historical Quarterly, 38 (April, 1960), 280-293.

See also 229.

TALLAHASSEE

226 Estes, Maxie C. "A Century of Theatre Activity in the Capital City of Florida: A Historical Study of Theatrical Entertainment in Tallahassee, Florida, from 1857 to 1957. " Ph. D. Florida State University, 1962. 364 p. [63-01809]

227 West, William Russell. "An Historical Study of Pro-
      fessional Theatre Activities in Tallahassee, Florida,
      from January, 1874 to November, 1893. " M. S.
      Florida State University, 1954. 103 p.

228 Meginnis, Ben A., Sr. "Munro's Opera House. " Ap-
      alachee, 5 (1957-1962), 72-75.

See also 229.

GENERAL

229 Dodd, William G. "Theatrical Entertainment in Early
      Florida. " Florida Historical Quarterly, 25 (October,
      1946), 121-174. (Apalachicola, Pensacola, St. Aug-
      ustine, Tallahassee) (1821-1844)

GEORGIA

ATHENS

230 Maxwell, Bernice June. "An Historical Survey of the
      Non-Professional Theatrical Activities at the Uni-
      versity of Georgia from 1785 through 1955. " M. F. A.
      University of Georgia, 1956.

231 Knight, Virginia D. "The New Opera House of Athens,
      Georgia, 1887-1932. " M. F. A. University of Georgia,
      1970.

ATLANTA

232 Barker, Meta. "Some Highlights of the Old Atlanta
      Stage. " Atlanta Historical Bulletin, 1 (January,
      1928), 33-50. (1855-1881)

233 Perkerson, Angus. "Famous American Theatres. "
      Theatre Arts, 41 (March, 1957), 63, 93. (1893-)

234 Hornady, John R. "The Stage--Now and Then. " At-
      lanta Yesterday, Today and Tomorrow. Atlanta,
      Georgia, 1922.

AUGUSTA

235 Wagner, John W. "Some Early Musical Moments in
     Augusta. " Georgia Historical Quarterly, 56 (Winter,
     1972), 529-534. (1819-1823)

COLUMBUS

236 Langley, William Osler.   "The Theatre in Columbus,
     Georgia, 1828-1878. " M. S. Auburn University,
     1937. 215 p.

237 Keller, Helen B.   "Eight Theaters in Columbus Since
     the City Came into Existence. " Industrial Index,
     April 22, 1959, p. 35.

     See also 1471.

MACON

     See 1427.

SAVANNAH

238 Bragg, Lillian Chaplin, and Margaret Walton Godley.
     Stories of Old Savannah, First Series ... with a
     Special Article on the Savannah Theatre by Charles
     Coburn. Savannah, Ga. , 1948. 35 p. (1736-1931)

239 Patrick, John Max. Savannah's Pioneer Theater from
     Its Origins to 1810. Athens: University of Georgia
     Press, 1953. 94 p. (1781-)

240 Sparks, Andrew. "A History of the Theatre in Savan-
     nah, 1800-1836. " M. A. University of Georgia, 1940.

241 Green, Elvena Marion.   "Theatre and Other Entertain-
     ments in Savannah, Georgia, from 1810 to 1865. "
     Ph. D. University of Iowa, 1971. 2 vols. 601 p.
     [72-08255]

242 Armistead, Margaret Beauchamp.   "The Savannah The-
     ater--Oldest in America. " The Georgia Review, 7
     (Spring, 1953), 50-55. (1818-1953)

243 Morehouse, Ward. "Famous American Theatres. "
     Theatre Arts, 41 (July, 1957), 33. (1818-)

244 Speaight, George. "An English Scene Painter in Amer-
     ica. " Theatre Notebook, 10 (July-September, 1956),
     122-124. (1819)

245 Hester, Wyoline. "The Savannah Stage. " M. A. Auburn
     University, 1930. 190 p. (-1865)

246 Overstreet, Robert Lane. "The History of the Savannah
     Theatre, 1865-1906. " Ph. D. Louisiana State Uni-
     versity, 1970. 2 vols. vi, 521 p. [71-03431]

247 _____. "John T. Ford and the Savannah Theater. "
     Southern Speech Communication Journal, 38 (Fall,
     1972), 51-60. (1869-1894)

248 _____. "Joseph Jefferson, Rip Van Winkle, and
     Savannah. " Georgia Speech Journal, 3 (Fall, 1971),
     28-39. (1873-1903)

249 Coburn, Charles. "Within These Walls. " Theatre
     Annual, 1 (1942), 29-36. (1890's)

250 Overstreet, Robert. "Sarah Bernhardt in Savannah. "
     Western Speech, 39 (Winter, 1975), 20-25. (1892,
     1906)

     See also 1408, 1427.

GENERAL

251 Gowart, Ellen Rambo. "Fanny Kemble in Georgia. "
     Georgia Review, 8 (Fall, 1954), 324-330. (1838-
     1839)

252 Cate, Margaret Davis. "Mistakes in Fanny Kemble's
     Georgia Journal. " Georgia Historical Quarterly, 44
     (March, 1960), 1-17. (1838-1839)

253 Scott, John A. "On the Authenticity of Fanny Kemble's
     Journal of a Residence on a Georgian Plantation in
     1838-1839. " Journal of Negro History, 44 (October,
     1961), 233-242.

254 Fife, Iline. "The Confederate Theater in Georgia. "
     Georgia Review, 9 (Fall, 1955), 305-315. (1860-
     1864)

255 Nolan, Paul T. "Georgia Drama between the Wars
       (1870-1916): A Check List. " Georgia Historical
       Quarterly, 51 (June, 1967), 216-230.

     See also 1426, 1442.

HAWAII

HONOLULU

256 Hoyt, Helen Peterson. "Theatre in Hawaii--1778-1840. "
       Hawaiian Historical Society Annual Report for 1960,
       Vol. 69. Honolulu, 1961. pp. 7-19.

257 Sheldon, Henry L. "Reminiscences of Theatricals in
       Honolulu. " Hawaiian Almanac and Annual for 1881,
       Vol. 7. Honolulu, 1880. pp. 34-39. (1847-1880)

258 "Reminiscences of the Stage in Honolulu. " Hawaiian
       Almanac and Annual for 1906, Vol. 32. Honolulu,
       1905. pp. 93-104.

259 Wilson, William F. "Professor John Henry Anderson
       'The Wizard of the North' at Honolulu in 1859. "
       Hawaiian Historical Society Annual Report for 1938.
       Honolulu, 1939. pp. 50-70.

260 Brown, Thelma Coile. "A History of the Theatre in
       Honolulu during the Reign of Kamehameha V, 1863-
       1872. " M. A. University of Hawaii, 1942.

261 Topham, Helen Arlington. "A History of the Theatre in
       Honolulu, 1891-1900. " M. A. University of Hawaii,
       1950.

262 MacGuigan, J. Roger. [Series of articles on the history
       of the theater in Honolulu], Honolulu Advertiser,
       March 3, 1929, sec. 3, p. 13; March 4, 1929, p.
       7; March 5, 1929, p. 5; March 6, 1929, p. 7.

GENERAL

263 Mellen, George. "Lights! and Give 'Em a Hand: The-

atrical Enterprise in Hawaii Traced from a First
Night in 1810 to date...," Sales Builder, 10 (January, 1937), 1-13. (1810-1936)

264 Wilson, Willard. "The Theatre in Hawaii before 1900."
     Quarterly Journal of Speech, 35 (October, 1949),
     304-309. (1847-1900)

265 Frowe, Margaret Mary. "The History of the Theatre
     during the Reign of King Kalakaua, 1874-1891."
     M. A. University of Hawaii, 1937.

IDAHO

BOISE

266 Eggers, Robert Franklin. "A History of Theatre in
     Boise, Idaho from 1863 to 1963." M. A. University
     of Oregon, 1963. 201 p. [M-491]

267 Hiatt, Richard Gordon. "A History of Theatrical Ac-
     tivity on the Oregon Trail (Boise, Idaho, to The
     Dalles, Oregon: 1880-1910)." Ph. D. Brigham
     Young University, 1974. 363 p. [74-17934]

268 Donaldson, Thomas. Idaho of Yesterday. Caldwell,
     Idaho: The Caxton Printers, Ltd. , 1941. pp. 104-
     109.

269 Hall, Utahna. "The Theatre Came to Boise by Pack
     Train." Idaho Daily Statesman, January 21, 1940,
     sec. 2, p. 12.

270 _____. "Boise Theatre Had Gay Times before
     Movies." Idaho Daily Statesman, February 11, 1940,
     sec. 2, p. 14.

See also 274, 1457.

CALDWELL

See 274.

EAGLE ROCK

See 274.

IDAHO CITY

271 Gilliard, Frederick W. "Pioneer Dramatists in the
     Boise Basin. " Idaho Yesterdays, 19, No. 4 (1976),
     2-9. (1864-1866)

     See also 274, 1457.

KETCHUM

See 274.

POCATELLO

272 Averett, Richard A. "History of the Auditorium Theatre
     in Pocatello, Idaho from 1893 to 1939. " M. A. Idaho
     State University, 1970.

SILVER CITY

273 Gilliard, Frederick W. "Early Theatre in the Owyhees. "
     Idaho Yesterdays, 17 (Summer, 1973), 9-15. (1866-
     1874)

     See also 274.

GENERAL

274 Gilliard, Frederick W. "Theatre in Early Idaho: A
     Brief Review and Appraisal. " Rendezvous, 8 (1973),
     25-31. (Boise, Caldwell, Eagle Rock, Idaho City,
     Ketchum, Silver City) (1860's-)

     See also 1456.

ILLINOIS

ALTON

See 335.

BEARDSTOWN

275 Sozen, Joyce Lorraine Chalcraft. "Annals of the Opera
      House in Beardstown, Illinois, from 1872-1900. "
      M. A. University of Illinois, Urbana, 1957. 158 p.

BLOOMINGTON

276 Drexler, Ralph Duane. "A History of the Theatre in
      Bloomington, Illinois, from Its Beginning to 1873. "
      M. S. Illinois State University, Normal, 1963. 134 p.
      (1850-)

277 Wilson, Robert. "A History of Professional Theatre in
      Bloomington, Illinois from 1874 through 1896. " M. S.
      Illinois State University, Normal, 1967.

CAIRO

278 Briggs, Harold Edward. 'Floating Circuses. " Egyptian
      Key, 3 (September, 1951), 19-23. (1848-1858)

279 _____ . "Entertainment and Amusement in Cairo,
      1848-1858. " Journal of the Illinois State Historical
      Society, 47 (Autumn, 1954), 231-251.

280 Stallings, Roy. "The Drama in Southern Illinois (1865-
      1900). " Journal of the Illinois State Historical So-
      ciety, 33 (June, 1940), 190-202.

CARBONDALE

281 Brown, James L. "Theatre at Southern Illinois Uni-
      versity, 1893-1966: A History. " M. S. Southern
      Illinois University, Carbondale, 1966.

CARROLLTON

      See 335.

CHAMPAIGN

      See 336.

CHICAGO

282 Briggs, Harold Edward, and Ernestine B. Briggs. "The
      Early Theatre in Chicago. " Journal of the Illinois

State Historical Society, 39 (June, 1946), 165-178. (1834-1857)

283 Sherman, Robert Lowery. Chicago Stage, Its Records and Achievements. Chicago, 1947. (1837-1871)

284 Van Kirk, Gordon. "The Beginnings of the Theatre in Chicago, 1837-1839. " M. A. Northwestern University, 1934. 72 p.

285 Day, Myrle. "The History of the Theatre of Chicago. " M. A. University of Northern Colorado, 1942. (1837-1940)

286 Oman, Richard J. "Chicago Theatre 1837-1847: Reflections of an Emerging Metropolis. " M. A. University of Florida, 1970. 112 p.

287 Bergfald, Milburn John. "Productions of Shakespeare in Chicago, 1837-1857. " M. A. Northwestern University, 1936.

288 Freiberger, Edward. "Theatre Beginnings in Chicago. " The Theatre, 13 (June, 1911), 198-200. (1837-)

289 Wilt, James Napier. "The History of the Two Rice Theatres in Chicago from 1847 to 1857. " Ph. D. University of Chicago, 1923. 463 p.

290 Sturtevant, Catherine. "A Study of the Dramatic Productions of Two Decades in Chicago: 1847-1857, and 1897-1907. " Ph. D. University of Chicago, 1931. 385 p.

291 Olson, Esther Marie. "The German Theater in Chicago During the Nineteenth Century. " M. A. Northwestern University, 1932.

292 Dummer, Esther Olson. "The German Theater in Chicago. " Jahrbuch der Deutsch-Amerikanischen Gesellschaft von Illinois, 33 (1937), 68-123. (1852-1934)

293 Andreas, Alfred Theodore. "The Drama, Music, Literature and Art. " History of Chicago. Chicago: A. T. Andreas, 1884. Vol. 1, pp. 472-506. (-1857)

294 _____. "The Drama." History of Chicago. Chi-
     cago: A. T. Andreas, 1885. Vol. 2, pp. 596-613.
     (1857-1871); Vol. 3, pp. 657-672. (1871-1885)

295 Ludwig, Jay Ferris. "McVicker's Theatre, 1857-1896."
     Ph. D. University of Illinois, Urbana, 1958. v, 143
     p. [58-05448]

296 _____. "James H. McVicker and His Theatre."
     Quarterly Journal of Speech, 46 (February, 1960),
     14-25. (1857-1896)

297 Bergstrom, Lois Mildred. "The History of the Mc-
     Vicker's Theatre, 1857-1861." M. A. University of
     Chicago, 1930. 313 p.

298 Thorson, Lillian Theodore. "A Record of the First
     Year of McVicker's Theater, November 7, 1857-
     November 7, 1858." M. A. University of Michigan,
     Ann Arbor, 1946. 122 p.

299 "A Historic Play House." The Dramatic Magazine, 2
     (November, 1897), 37-40. (1857-1897)

300 Renner, Richard Wilson. "Ye Kort Martial: A Tale of
     Chicago Politics, Theatre, Journalism, and Militia."
     Journal of Illinois State Historical Society, 66 (Win-
     ter, 1973), 376-386. (1858)

301 Wilt, Napier, and Henriette C. Koren Naeseth. "Two
     Early Norwegian Dramatic Societies in Chicago."
     Norwegian-American Studies and Records, 11 (1938),
     44-75. (1860-1880)

302 Cooper, Allen R. "Colonel Wood's Museum: A Study
     in the Development of the Early Chicago Stage."
     M. A. Roosevelt University, 1974. (1864-1871)

303 Albert, Bessie. "Reminiscences of Western Theatres:
     The Crosby Opera House, Chicago." Dramatic Mag-
     azine, 1 (August, 1880), 347-349. (1865-1871)

304 Hansen, Harry. "How to Give Away an Opera House."
     Journal of the Illinois State Historical Society, 39
     (December, 1946), 419-424. (1865-1867)

305 Wright, James W. "The Chicago Auditorium Theatre:
     1866-1966." M. A. Michigan State University, 1966.

306 Naeseth, Henriette C. K. The Swedish Theatre of Chicago, 1868-1950. Rock Island, Ill.: Augustana Historical Society, 1951. 390 p.

307 _____. "Drama in Swedish in Chicago." Journal of Illinois State Historical Society, 41 (June, 1948), 159-170. (1868-1913)

308 Lindblom, Ernst. Svenska Teaterminnen från Chicago. Stockholm: C. L. Gullberg, 1916. 192 p.

309 Walker, William S. The Chicago Stage: Containing Sketches of the Prominent Members of the Local Amusement Profession, for the Season, 1870-1871. Chicago: Horton and Leonard, 1871. 61 p.

310 Johnson, Genevieve Goodman. "A History of the Chicago Theater, October 21, 1871-1872." M. A. University of Chicago, 1932.

311 Glover, Lyman Beecher. The Story of a Theatre. Chicago: R. R. Donnelley and Sons, 1898. 129 p. (1871-1898)

312 Photographic Diagrams: Description and Location of the Theaters and Halls of Chicago. 1st Ed. Chicago: J. H. Hunter, 1875. 27 p.

313 Shiffler, Harrold C. "The Chicago Church-Theater Controversy of 1881-1882." Journal of the Illinois State Historical Society, 53 (Winter, 1960), 361-375.

314 Hupp, Sandra. "Chicago's Church-Theatre Controversy." Players, 46 (December, 1970-January, 1971), 60-64. (1881-1882)

315 McVicker, James Hubert. The Theatre; Its Early Days in Chicago: A Paper Read before the Chicago Historical Society, February 19, 1884. Chicago: Knight, 1884. 88 p.

316 Denson, Wilbur Thurman. "A History of the Chicago Auditorium." Ph. D. University of Wisconsin, Madison, 1974. 278 p. [74-19328] (1889-1973)

317 Flynn, Ruth. "A Historical Study of Dramatic Activities for Children at Hull House Theatre, Chicago, Illinois, from 1889-1967." M. A. University of Denver, 1967.

318   Pelham, Laura Dainty.   "The Story of the Hull-House
      Players. "   The Drama, 6 (May, 1916), 249-262.

319   Phelps, Albert D.   "How the Hull House Players
      Fought Their Way to Success. "   The Theatre, 20
      (November, 1914), 229-232, 239.

320   "The Alhambra of Chicago. "   Dramatic Magazine, 2
      (December, 1897-January, 1898), 153-158.   (1891-
      1897)

321   Moses, John, and Joseph Kirkland.   History of Chicago,
      Illinois.   Chicago: Munsell & Co. , 1895.   Vol. 2,
      pp. 565-577.

322   Nixon, Charles E.   "Epitome of Chicago's Theatrical
      History. "   Illinois Theatre Souvenir Programme.
      Chicago: Rand, McNally & Co. , 1900.   pp. 23-45.

      See also 335.

DECATUR

323   Richmond, Mabel E.   Centennial History of Decatur and
      Macon County.   Decatur: The Decatur Review, 1930.
      Chapter 43, "Theatres-Clubs. "

      See also 336.

GALENA

324   Wilmeth, Don B.   "The MacKenzie-Jefferson Theatrical
      Company in Galena, 1838-1839. "   Journal of the
      Illinois State Historical Society, 60 (Spring, 1967),
      23-36.

      See also 335, 1446.

HIGHLAND

325   Ott, Pamela Worley.   "A Comparative Study of Drama,
      Art, Music, and Dance in Highland, Illinois. "   M. S.
      Southern Illinois University, Carbondale, 1971.
      Chapter 2, pp. 4-34.   (1830's-)

JACKSONVILLE

      See 335.

JOLIET

See 335.

NORMAL

326 Carpenter, Barbara Louise. "A History of Theatre at Illinois State Normal University, 1857-1959. " M. A. Illinois State University, Normal, 1964.

OTTOWA

See 335.

PEKIN

See 335.

PEORIA

327 Marine, Don. "A History of Professional Stage Theatricals in Peoria, Illinois Before the Civil War. " Ph. D. Tulane University, 1972. 323 p. [72-24412] (1838-1860)

328 Reed, Carole Fay. "A History of the Grand Opera House in Peoria, Illinois. " M. S. Illinois State University, Normal, 1963. (1882-1909)

See also 335.

PERU

See 335.

QUINCY

See 336.

SPRINGFIELD

329 House, Henry B. "History of Spoken Drama on Springfield Stage for Last 92 Years. " Illinois Libraries, 12 (October, 1930), 95-101. (1838-)

330 "Stage History Here Dates Back 98 Years. " Illinois State Register Centennial Edition 1836-1936. June 28, 1936, Commercial sec. , p. 11.

331   Hemminger, Art. "Mr. Lincoln Goes to the Theatre."
      Journal of the Illinois State Historical Society, 33
      (December, 1940), 469-477. (1839-)

332   Yonick, Cora Jane. "A History of the Theatre in
      Springfield, Illinois, from 1855 to 1876." M. A. Uni-
      versity of Wyoming, 1952. 120 p.

333   Bunn, George W., Jr. "The Old Chatterton: A Brief
      History of a Famous Old Opera House." Journal of
      the Illinois State Historical Society, 36 (March, 1943),
      7-20. (1866-1924)

      See also 335, 336.

URBANA

334   Homrighous, Mary Elizabeth. "A History of Non-Pro-
      fessional Theatrical Production at the University of
      Illinois from Its Beginning to 1923." M. A. Uni-
      versity of Illinois, Urbana, 1949. (1872-)

      See also 336.

GENERAL

335   Farrell, Robert Dale. "The Illinois Theatrical Company,
      1837-1840." M. A. University of Illinois, Urbana,
      1964. 101 p.

336   Donahoe, Ned. "Theatres in Central Illinois--1850-
      1900." Ph. D. University of Illinois, Urbana, 1953.
      iii, 80 p. [00-05954] (Champaign, Decatur, Quincy,
      Springfield, Urbana)

INDIANA

BLOOMINGTON

337   Cope, Garrett Livingston, Jr. "History of the Origin
      and Development of Theatre Arts at Indiana Uni-
      versity." M. A. Indiana University, 1951. v, .331
      p. (1896-1950)

EVANSVILLE

338 Schluessler, Douglas. "Evansville's Early Major Theatres From 1868 to 1915. " M. A. Indiana University,
1968.

FT. WAYNE

339 Tolan, Robert Warren. "A History of the Legitimate,
Professional Theatre in Ft. Wayne, Indiana from
1854-1884. " Ph. D. Purdue University, 1968. vi,
337 p. [69-02987]

340 Slattery, Kenneth Martin. "A History of Theatrical
Activity in Fort Wayne, Indiana with Emphasis on
the Professional Theatre, 1884-1905. " Ph. D. Kent
State University, 1973. 2 vols. 1035 p. [73-32358]

GREENCASTLE

341 Brock, Richard Barrett. "A Study of the Greencastle,
Indiana, Opera House, 1875-1912. " M. A. DePauw
University, 1963.

342 Clithero, Edith Patricia. "History of Dramatic Activity
at DePauw University. " M. A. DePauw University,
1957.

343 "Theatre Activities at DePauw University. " Players
Magazine, 21 (April, 1945), 17. (1881-)

INDIANAPOLIS

344 Scott, Davis A. "'Oh Thou Corrupter of Youth': Henry
Ward Beecher vs. Indianapolis Theatre. " Central
State Speech Journal, 14 (February, 1963), 17-22.
(1823-1843)

345 Draegert, Eva. "The Theater in Indianapolis before
1880. " Indiana Magazine of History, 51 (June, 1955),
121-138. (1868-1879)

346 Gooch, D. H. "A History of the Stage in Indianapolis
from 1875 to 1890. " M. A. University of Iowa, 1932.
2 vols.

347 Knaub, Richard Keith. "The History of English's Opera
     House and the English Theatre. " Ph. D. Indiana Uni-
     versity, 1962. 399 p. [63-2871] (1880-1948)

348 Draegert, Eva. "Cultural History of Indianapolis: The
     Theater, 1880-1890. " Indiana Magazine of History,
     52 (March, 1956), 21-48.

349 Sullivan, William George. "English's Opera House. "
     Indiana Historical Society Publications, Vol. 20,
     No. 3 (1960), pp. 333-378. (1880-1948)

350 Byram, John. "Famous American Theatres. " Theatre
     Arts, 42 (October, 1958), 24-25, 78-79. (1880-)

351 Sulgrove, Berry R. History of Indianapolis and Marion
     County, Indiana. Philadelphia, 1884. pp. 256-261.

352 Schaub, Owen W. "A History of the Grand Opera
     House Stock Company of Indianapolis, 1898 to 1900. "
     M. A. Indiana University, 1968.

353 Dunn, Jacob Piatt. Greater Indianapolis: The History,
     the Industries, the Institutions, and the People of a
     City of Homes. Indianapolis, Ind. : Lewis Publish-
     ing Co. , 1910. Vol. 1, Chapter 36, "The Theatre
     and Theatricals. "

NEW HARMONY

354 Weinfeld, Samuel L. "A Survey of Early Theatrical
     Activity at New Harmony, Indiana. " M. A. Indiana
     University, 1964. 103 p. (1828-)

     See also 1471.

SOUTH BEND

355 Chreist, Frederick Martin. "The History of Profes-
     sional Theatre in South Bend, Indiana. " M. A.
     Northwestern University, 1937. (1831-1935)

TERRE HAUTE

356 Hanners, John. "Early Entertainments in Terre Haute,
     Indiana 1810-1865. " M. A. Indiana State University,
     1973. 139 p.

357   Lambert, Marlene Kalbfleisch. "The Terre Haute Opera
        House from 1869 until 1874. " M. A. Indiana State
        University, 1972.

358   Giglio, Mary Elena. "The Terre Haute Grand Opera
        House, 1897-1898. " M. A. Indiana State University,
        1974.

VINCENNES

359   Constantine, J. Robert. "Frontier Culture: The The-
        atre in Early Vincennes. " Old Northwest, 2 (1976),
        21-36. (1814-1838)

GENERAL

360   Stephenson, Robert Rex. "The Premier Season of
        Wysor's Grand Opera House, 1892-1893. " M. A.
        Indiana State University, 1972.

IOWA

BEDFORD

361   Mahan, Bruce E. "Pleasant Hill Dramatics. " Palimp-
        sest, 4 (January, 1923), 25-29. (1886-1887)

BURLINGTON

362   Ekdale, Edith Harper. "The Grand Opera House. "
        Palimpsest, 28 (June, 1947), 184-192. (1881-1940)

CEDAR RAPIDS

363   Lawrence, Charles A. Pioneer Days in Cedar Rapids,
        1860-1880. Cedar Rapids, 1936. pp. 148-158.

364   Griffith, Martha E. "The Czechs in Cedar Rapids:
        Dramatic Organizations. " Iowa Journal of History
        and Politics, 42 (1944), 144-147. (1869-1902)

365 Murray, Janette Stevenson, and Frederick Gray Murray.
     The Story of Cedar Rapids. New York: Stratford
     House, 1950. pp. 223-234.

See also 383.

DAVENPORT

366 Schick, Joseph S. "Cultural Beginnings and the Rise of
     the Theatre, German and American, in Eastern Iowa
     (Davenport) 1836-1863. " Ph. D. University of Chicago,
     1937. 384 p.

367 _____. The Early Theater in Eastern Iowa: Cul-
     tural Beginnings and the Rise of the Theater in Dav-
     enport and Eastern Iowa, 1836-1863. Chicago:
     University of Chicago Press, 1939. 384 p.

368 _____. "The Early Theater in Davenport. " Palimp-
     sest, 31 (January, 1950), 1-44. (1851-1862)

369 Richter, August Paul. Das Deutsche Theater in Daven-
     port, Iowa 1855-1905. Davenport: H. Lischer
     Printing Co. , 1906. 30 p.

370 Fay, Barbara Carleen Brice. "The Theatre in South-
     eastern Iowa, 1864-1880. " M. A. University of Iowa,
     1947. 176 p.

371 Brice, Barbara. "The Amateur Theatre in Iowa Life. "
     Mid-America, 31 (October, 1949), 248-257. (1864-
     1880)

See also 1446.

DES MOINES

372 Lewison, Agnes O. "A Theatrical History of Des
     Moines, Iowa, 1846-1890. " M. A. University of
     Iowa, 1931. 277 p.

373 Payne, W. O. "Moore's Opera House. " Annals of
     Iowa, 17 (January, 1930), 163-167. (picture only,
     p. 162) (1870's)

See also 1446.

DUBUQUE

374 Geroux, Charles L. "The History of Theatres and Re-
     lated Theatrical Activity in Dubuque, Iowa, 1837-
     1877. " Ph. D. Wayne State University, 1973. 2 vols.
     vi, 611 p. [74-11101]

375 Mahan, Bruce E. "The Iowa Thespians. " Palimpsest,
     4 (January, 1923), 14-24. (1838-)

376 Kintzle, Clarence A. "The Julien Theatre. " Palimp-
     sest, 15 (April, 1934), 139-158. (1856-1870)

377 Kelm, William Eulberg. "The People's Theatre. " Pa-
     limpsest, 9 (March, 1928), 89-105. (1857-1859)

     See also 335, 383, 1446.

HAMPTON

378 Sweet, Oney Fred. "The Opera House. " Iowa Journal
     of History and Politics, 38 (1940), 346-355.

KEOKUK

379 Hamilton, Robert T. "A History of Theatre in Keokuk,
     Iowa, from 1875 to 1900. " M. A. University of
     Michigan, Ann Arbor, 1954.

SIOUX CITY

380 Willson, Loretta Lyle. "A Survey of Dramatic Pro-
     ductions on the Legitimate Stage in Sioux City, Iowa,
     1870-1919. " M. A. Northwestern University, 1936.

     See also 383, 1447.

GENERAL

381 Wegelin, Oscar. "An Early Iowa Playwright. " New
     York Historical Society Quarterly Bulletin, 28 (April,
     1944), 42-44. (1869-1870)

382 Mahan, Bruce E. "At the Opera House. " Palimpsest,
     5 (November, 1924), 408-423. (1884-1885)

383 Funk, Nancy Louise.   "Professional Theatrical Activity
     in Iowa from 1890 to 1895. " M. A. University of
     Iowa, 1966.   (Cedar Rapids, Dubuque, Sioux City)

     See also 1450, 1472.

KANSAS

ABILENE

     See 397.

ATCHISON

     See 397, 398.

CONCORDIA

384 Doyen, Peggy J.   "The History of Theater 1878-1925
     in Concordia, Kansas. " M. A. Kansas State Univer-
     sity, 1969.   120 p.

DODGE CITY

385 Malin, James Claude.   "Dodge City Varieties--A Summer
     Interlude of Entertainment, 1878. " Kansas Histor-
     ical Quarterly, 22 (Winter, 1956), 347-353.

386 Maloney, Martin J.   "The Frontier Theatre. " Players
     Magazine, 15 (July-August, 1939), 6; 16 (October,
     1939), 6; (November, 1939), 6; (December, 1939),
     6.   (1878-1879)

     See also 397.

ELLSWORTH

387 Prouty, S. S.   "When Ellsworth Catered to the Texas
     Trade. " Kansas Historical Quarterly, 18 (August,
     1950), 325-328.   (1873)

     See also 397.

EMPORIA

388 Kemmerling, James. "A History of the Whitley Opera
     House in Emporia, Kansas: 1881-1913. " M. S.
     Emporia State University, 1967.

     See also 397.

FORT ATKINSON

389 Ivey, Zida C. "Early Theatres in Fort Atkinson. "
     Wisconsin Stage, 8 (Winter, 1954-1955), 8-10.

FORT RILEY

     See 397.

FORT SCOTT

390 Malin, James Claude. "Early Theatre at Fort Scott. "
     Kansas Historical Quarterly, 24 (Spring, 1958), 31-
     56. (1862-1874)

     See also 397.

GARDEN CITY

391 Fowler, Larry. "History of the Stevens Opera House,
     Garden City, Kansas, 1886-1929. " M. S. Emporia
     State University, 1969.

HAYS

     See 397.

HUTCHINSON

     See 397.

JUNCTION CITY

392 Jonason, Marvin G. "A History of the Junction City
     Opera House in Junction City, Kansas: 1880-1919. "
     M. S. Emporia State University, 1970.

LAWRENCE

393 Birner, Mona. "A Chronological Record of Theatrical

Activities in Lawrence, Kansas, between 1879 and
1911 as Reported in the Lawrence Newspapers. "
M. A. University of Kansas, 1962.

394 Le Ban, Frank Kenneth. "A History of Theatre Acti-
     vities at the University of Kansas. " M. A. Univer-
     sity of Kansas, 1959. (1884-1956)

     See also 398.

LEAVENWORTH

395 Malin, James C. "Theatre in Kansas, 1858-1868:
     Background for the Coming of the Lord Dramatic
     Company to Kansas, 1869. " Kansas Historical Quar-
     terly, 23 (Spring, 1957), 10-53.

     See also 397.

NEWTON

     See 397.

TOPEKA

     See 397, 398.

WICHITA

396 Mather, Patricia Ann. "The Theatrical History of
     Wichita, Kansas, 1872-1920. " M. A. University of
     Kansas, 1950.

GENERAL

397 Meltzer, George. "Social Life and Entertainment on the
     Frontiers of Kansas, 1854-1890. " M. A. Wichita State
     University, 1941. (drama pages 138-175) (Abilene,
     Atchison, Dodge City, Ellsworth, Emporia, Fort
     Riley, Fort Scott, Hays, Hutchinson, Leavenworth,
     Newton, Topeka)

398 Malin, James C. "Theatre in Kansas, 1858-1868: Back-
     ground for the Coming of the Lord Dramatic Company
     to Kansas, 1869, --Concluded. " Kansas Historical
     Quarterly, 23 (Summer, 1957), 191-203. (Atchison,
     Lawrence, Topeka) (1866-)

399 _____. "Traveling Theatre in Kansas: The James
         A. Lord Chicago Dramatic Company, 1869-1871. "
         Kansas Historical Quarterly, 23 (Autumn, 1957), 298-
         323; (Winter, 1957), 401-438.

400 _____. "James A. and Louie Lord: Theatrical
         Team: Their Personal Story, 1869-1889. " Kansas
         Historical Quarterly, 22 (Autumn, 1956), 242-275.

KENTUCKY

LEXINGTON

401 Weisert, John J. "Beginnings of the Kentucky Theatre
         Circuit. " Filson Club History Quarterly, 34 (July,
         1960), 264-285. (1790-1818)

402 Langworthy, Helen. "The Theater in the Frontier
         Cities of Lexington, Kentucky, and Cincinnati, Ohio,
         1797-1835. " Ph. D. University of Iowa, 1952. 339
         p. [00-04079]

403 Meek, Beryl. "A Record of the Stage in Lexington,
         Kentucky, 1799-1850. " M. A. University of Iowa,
         1930.

404 Clay, Lucille Noff. "The Lexington Theatre from 1800
         to 1840. " M. A. University of Kentucky, 1930.

405 Crum, Mabel Irene Tyree. "The History of the Lex-
         ington Theater from the Beginning to 1860. " Ph. D.
         University of Kentucky, 1956. 2 vols. v, 667 p.
         [61-00293] (1808-)

406 Arnold, John Coleman. "A History of the Lexington
         Theatre from 1887 to 1900. " Ph. D. University of
         Kentucky, 1956. iv, 433 p. [61-00291]

         See also 424, 932.

LOUISVILLE

407 Jones, Jane Eleanor. "History of the Stage in Louis-

ville, Kentucky from Its Beginning to 1855. " M. A.
University of Iowa, 1932. (1808-)

408 Dietz, Mary Martha. "The History of the Theater in
Louisville. " M. A. University of Louisville, 1921.

409 Weisert, John Jacob. The Curtain Rose: A Checklist
of Performances at Samuel Drake's City Theatre and
Other Theatres at Louisville from the Beginning to
1843. Louisville, Kentucky, 1958. 183 p. (1811-)

410 _____ . "The First Decade at Sam Drake's Louisville Theatre. " Filson Club History Quarterly, 39
(October, 1965), 287-310. (1819-1829)

411 _____ . "The Chief Competitor of Drake's City Theatre. " Register of the Kentucky Historical Society,
66 (April, 1968), 159-167. (1829-1840)

412 _____ . "Golden Days at Drake's City Theatre, 1830-
1833. " Filson Club History Quarterly, 43 (July,
1969), 255-270.

413 _____ . "An End and Several Beginnings: The Passing of Drake's City Theatre. " Filson Club History
Quarterly, 50 (January, 1976), 5-28. (1833-1842)

414 _____ . A Large and Fashionable Audience: A
Checklist of Performances at the Louisville Theatre,
1846-1866. Louisville, Ky. , 1955. 223 p.

415 _____ . "Beginnings of German Theatricals in Louisville. " Filson Club History Quarterly, 26 (October,
1952), 347-359. (1850-1854)

416 _____ . Mozart Hall, 1851 to 1866: A Checklist of
Attractions at a Minor Theatre of Louisville, Ken-
tucky, Known Variously as Mozart Hall, Wood's
Theatre, or The Academy of Music. Louisville,
Ky. , 1962. 82 p.

417 Hill, West Thompson, Jr. "A Study of the Macauley's
Theatre in Louisville, Kentucky, 1873-1880. " Ph. D.
University of Iowa, 1954. 2 vols. 482 p. [00-
07565]

418 _____. "Opening of Macauley's Theatre, Louisville, Kentucky, October 4, 1873. " Filson Club History Quarterly, 32 (April, 1958), 151-167.

419 _____. "Famous American Theatres. " Theatre Arts, 44 (February, 1960), 93-94. (1873-)

420 Combs, Don Whitney. "A History of Macauley's Theatre, Louisville, Kentucky, 1873-1925. " Ph. D. University of Illinois, Urbana, 1977. 154 p. [77-26652]

421 Weisert, John Jacob. Last Night at Macauley's: A Checklist, 1873-1925. Louisville: University of Louisville, 1950. 218 p.

422 Friedlander, Mitzi. "History of a Theater. " Filson Club History Quarterly, 45 (July, 1971), 305-314. (1894-)

See also 424, 932.

GENERAL

423 Hill, West T. , Jr. The Theatre in Early Kentucky: 1790-1820. Lexington: University Press of Kentucky, 1971. 205 p.

424 Clarke, Mitchell. "The History of the Early Theatre in Kentucky. " M. A. Western Kentucky University, 1936. (Lexington, Louisville) (1800-1850)

LOUISIANA

ALEXANDRIA

425 Gray, Wallace Allison. "The Professional Theatre in Alexandria, Louisiana, 1822-1920. " M. A. Louisiana State University, 1951. 249 p.

See also 517.

BATON ROUGE

426 Varnado, Alban Fordesh. "A History of Theatrical
      Activity in Baton Rouge, Louisiana, 1819-1900. "
      M. A. Louisiana State University, 1947.   95 p.

HOUMA

See 517.

NATCHITOCHES

427 Bridges, Katherine. "All Well in Natchitoches: A
      Louisiana City on the Stage. " Louisiana Studies, 10
      (Summer, 1971), 85-91.   (1823)

NEW ORLEANS

428 Wright, Harriette E.   (The stage in New Orleans, 1753-
      1810.) New York Dramatic Mirror, 50 (December 5,
      1903), 17.

429 Le Gardeur, René J. , Jr. "Les Premières Années du
      Théâtre à la Nouvelle-Orléans. " Athenée Louisianais
      Comptes Rendus, March, 1954, pp. 33-72.   (1789-
      1797)

430 Baroncelli, Joseph Gabriel de.   Année 1791.   Le Thé-
      âtre Français à la Nouvelle Orléans: Essai Histor-
      ique.   New Orleans: G. Muller, 1906.   112 p.

431 Nadeau, Gabriel. "Le Théâtre Chez les Franco-Amér-
      icains. " Bulletin de la Société Historique Franco-
      Américaine, 1 (1956), 69-74.

432 Lafargue, André. "Opera in New Orleans in Days of
      Yore. " Louisiana Historical Quarterly, 29 (July,
      1946), 660-678.   (1791-1919)

433 Loeb, Harry Brunswick. "The Opera in New Orleans:
      A Historical Sketch from the Earliest Days Through
      the Season of 1914-15. " Publication of the Louisiana
      Historical Society, 9 (1916), 29-41.

434 Le Gardeur, René J. , Jr. The First New Orleans
      Theatre, 1792-1803. New Orleans: Leeward Books,
      1963.   58 p.

435 Price, Nellie Warner. "Le Spectacle de la Rue St.
     Pierre. " Louisiana Historical Quarterly, 1 (January,
     1918), 215-223. (1793-1811)

436 Isaacs, Edith J. R. , and Rosamond Gilder. "Gallic
     Fire: The French Theatre in America. " Theatre
     Arts, 28 (August, 1944), 456-464. (1793-)

437 Gotthold, Rozel. "New Orleans' First Theatre. " The-
     atre, 28 (August, 1918), 100. (179?)

438 Lyle, Beverly Bayne. "A Detailed Study of the New
     Orleans Theatre from 1800-1825. " M. A. Louisiana
     State University, 1938.

439 Fossier, Albert Emile. New Orleans: The Glamour
     Period, 1800-1840. New Orleans: Pelican Publish-
     ing Co. , 1957. pp. 467-484.

440 Smither, Nelle Kroger. "A History of the English The-
     atre at New Orleans, 1806-1842. " Ph. D. University
     of Pennsylvania, 1942. 429 p.

441 _____. "A History of the English Theatre at New
     Orleans, 1806-1842. " Louisiana Historical Quarterly,
     28 (January, 1945), 85-276; (April, 1945), 361-572.

442 Kendall, John Smith. The Golden Age of the New Or-
     leans Theater. Baton Rouge: Louisiana State Uni-
     versity Press, 1952. 624 p. (1806-1906)

443 McCutcheon, Roger P. "The First English Plays in
     New Orleans. " American Literature, 11 (May, 1939),
     183-199. (1806-1819)

444 Roppolo, Joseph Patrick. "Local and Topical Plays in
     New Orleans, 1806-1865. " Tulane Studies in English,
     4 (1954), 91-124.

445 _____. "American Themes, Heroes, and History in
     the New Orleans Stage, 1806-1865. " Tulane Studies
     in English, 5 (1955), 151-181.

446 DeMetz, Ouida Kaye. "The Uses of Dance in the Eng-
     lish Language Theatres of New Orleans Prior to the
     Civil War, 1806-1861. " Ph. D. Florida State Uni-
     versity, 1975. v, 261 p. [75-17930]

447 Lyle, Beverly, and C. L. Shaver. "Early English Drama
     in New Orleans. " Quarterly Journal of Speech, 25
     (April, 1939), 305-309. (1811, 1817)

448 Morrow, Marguerite Hess. "A History of the English
     Stage in New Orleans from 1817-1837. " M. A. Uni-
     versity of Iowa, 1926.

449 Perkins, Mrs. Johnnie A. "Dramatic Productions in
     New Orleans from 1817 to 1861. " M. A. Louisiana
     State University, 1929.

450 Bogner, Howard Francis. "Sir Walter Scott in New Or-
     leans, 1818-1832. " M. A. Tulane University, 1937.

451 Bogner, Harold F. "Sir Walter Scott in New Orleans,
     1818-1832. " Louisiana Historical Quarterly, 21
     (April, 1938), 420-517.

452 Roppolo, Joseph Patrick. "Hamlet in New Orleans. "
     Tulane Studies in English, 6 (1956), 71-86. (1820-
     1865)

453 Hostetler, Paul Smith. "The Influence of New Orleans
     on Early Nineteenth Century Theatre. " Southern
     Speech Journal, 29 (Fall, 1963), 12-19. (1820-1850)

454 Burroughs, Patricia. "The Career of Jane Placide in
     New Orleans. " M. A. Louisiana State University,
     1970. (1822-1835)

455 Smither, Nelle. A History of the English Theatre at
     New Orleans, 1806-1842. Philadelphia, 1944. 49 p.
     (1827-1833)

456 Kendall, John S. "New Orleans Negro Minstrels. "
     Louisiana Historical Quarterly, 30 (January, 1947),
     128-148. (1827-)

457 Chevalley, Sylvie Bostsarron. "Le Théâtre d'Orléans
     en tournée dans les villes du Nord, 1827-1833. "
     Athénée Louisianais Comptes Rendus, 1955, pp. 27-
     71.

458 Hanley, Kathryn Tierney. "The Amateur Theater in
     New Orleans before 1835. " M. A. Tulane Univer-
     sity, 1940.

459 Niehaus, E. F. "Paddy on the Local Stage and in Humour: The Image of the Irish in New Orleans, 1830-1862. " Louisiana History, 5 (Spring, 1964), 117-134.

460 Roane, Andrea Theresa. "The Showboat as a Theatrical Institution in New Orleans: 1831-1940. " M. A. University of New Orleans, 1973. 35 p.

461 Roppolo, Joseph Patrick. "American Premieres of Two Shakespearean Plays in New Orleans: 'The Two Gentlemen of Verona' and 'Antony and Cleopatra. '" Tulane Studies in English, 7 (1957), 125-132. (1831, 1838)

462 Kendall, John Smith. "The American Siddons. " Louisiana Historical Quarterly, 28 (July, 1945), 922-940. (1832-1838)

463 Hebron, Mary Dorothy. "Sir Walter Scott in New Orleans, 1833-1850. " M. A. Tulane University, 1940.

464 Pickett, Charles H. "A History of the Non-Commercial Theatre in New Orleans, from 1835 to 1860. " M. A. Louisiana State University, 1959.

465 Leary, Lewis, and Arlin Turner. "John Howard Payne in New Orleans. " Louisiana Historical Quarterly, 31 (January, 1948), 110-122. (1835)

466 Gafford, Lucile. "Material Conditions in the Theatres of New Orleans before the Civil War. " M. A. University of Chicago, 1925.

467 _____. "A History of the St. Charles Theatre in New Orleans, 1835-43. " Ph. D. University of Chicago, 1930. 273 p.

468 _____. A History of the St. Charles Theatre in New Orleans, 1835-43. Chicago: University of Chicago Press, 1932. 38 p.

469 Smither, Nelle. "Charlotte Cushman's Apprenticeship in New Orleans. " Louisiana Historical Quarterly, 31 (October, 1948), 973-980. (1835-1836)

470 Turner, Vivian D. "The Stage in New Orleans, Louisiana, after 1837. " M. A. University of Iowa, 1929. (1836-1854)

471 Grima, Edgar. "Municipal Support of Theatres and
     Operas in New Orleans." Louisiana Historical So-
     ciety Publications, 9 (1916), 43-. (1836-)

472 Smith, William Isaac. "The Picayune as a Record of
     Literary History of the Early Victorian Period 1837-
     1847." M. A. Tulane University, 1938. (23 p. on
     drama)

473 DeMetz, Kaye. "Juvenile Dancers on New Orleans Sta-
     ges During the Early Nineteenth Century." Southern
     Theatre, 18 (Fall, 1975), 13-17. (1839-1860)

474 Moehlenbrock, Arthur Henry. "The German Drama on
     the New Orleans Stage." Ph. D. University of Iowa,
     1941. 366 p. (1839-1890)

475 _____. "The German Drama on the New Orleans
     Stage." Louisiana Historical Quarterly, 26 (April,
     1943), 361-627. (1839-1890)

476 Hamilton, Mary Lucille. "The Lyceum in New Orleans,
     1840-1860." M. A. Louisiana State University, 1948.

477 Ward, Willie Pauline. "English and American Plays in
     New Orleans, 1840-1850." M. A. University of Texas,
     Austin, 1940.

478 Beckham, John Lewis. "Dion Boucicault in New Or-
     leans, 1841-1864." M. A. Tulane University, 1954.

479 Roppolo, Joseph Patrick. "A History of the American
     Stage in New Orleans, 1842-1845." M. A. Tulane
     University, 1948.

480 Kendall, John Smith. "Joseph Jefferson in New Or-
     leans." Louisiana Historical Quarterly, 26 (October,
     1943), 1150-1167. (1842-1904)

481 Roppolo, Joseph Patrick. "A History of the English
     Language Theatre in New Orleans, 1845 to 1861."
     Ph. D. Tulane University, 1950. 3 vols. 964 p.

482 _____. "Audiences in New Orleans Theatres, 1845-
     1861." Tulane Studies in English, 2 (1950), 121-135.

483 Parsons, Bill. "The Histrionics." Southern Speech
     Journal, 27 (Fall, 1961), 68-73. (1848-1874)

484 Melebeck, Claude Bernard, Jr. "A History of the First and Second Varieties Theatres of New Orleans, Louisiana, 1849 to 1870." Ph. D. Louisiana State University, 1973. 2 vols. ix, 655 p. [74-07244]

485 Gaisford, John. The Drama in New Orleans. New Orleans: J.B. Steel, 1849; Cambridge, Mass. , 1924. 55 p.

486 Kling, Esther Louise. "The New Orleans Academy of Music Theatre, 1853-1861." M. A. Louisiana State University, 1960.

487 Nugent, Beatrice. "Benedict DeBar's Management of the St. Charles Theatre in New Orleans, Louisiana, 1853-1861." M. A. Louisiana State University, 1967.

488 Roppolo, Joseph Patrick. "Uncle Tom in New Orleans: Three Lost Plays." New England Quarterly, 27 (June, 1954), 213-226. (1854)

489 Kayman, Eleanor K. "Leisure Time Activities in New Orleans, 1855-1863." M. A. Tulane University, 1966. (25 p. on drama)

490 Bender, Lorelle Causey. "The French Opera House of New Orleans, 1859-1890." M. A. Louisiana State University, 1940.

491 Lafargue, André. "The New Orleans French Opera House: A Retrospect." Louisiana Historical Quarterly, 3 (July, 1920), 368-372. (1859-1919)

492 Curtis, N. C. "The French Opera House, 1859-1917." Western Architecture, 38 (January, 1929), 5-8.

493 Kendall, John Smith. "Patti in New Orleans." Southwest Review, 16 (1931), 460-468. (1860)

494 Reynolds, Ina C. "A History of the New Orleans Academy of Music Theatre, 1861-1869." M. A. Louisiana State University, 1964.

495 Somers, Dale A. "War and Play: The Civil War in New Orleans." Mississippi Quarterly, 26 (Winter, 1972-1973), 3-28.

496 "A Night in the Orleans Theatre. " Southern Literary
    Messenger, 37 (1863), 565-568.

497 Hargett, Sheila. "A Daybook and a History of the St.
    Charles Theatre, 1864-1868. " M. A. Louisiana State
    University, 1971.

498 Krestalude, James Andrew. "A Daybook and a History
    of the St. Charles Theatre, 1868-1872. " M. A. Lou-
    isiana State University, 1972.

499 Boyd, Theodore Edward. "A History of the New Orleans
    Academy of Music Theatre, 1869-1880. " M. A. Lou-
    isiana State University, 1965.

500 Harrison, Shirley Madeline. "The Grand Opera House
    (Third Varieties Theatre) of New Orleans, Louisiana,
    1871 to 1906: A History and Analysis. " Ph. D. Lou-
    isiana State University, 1965. 4 vols. xxxiii, 1387 p.
    [65-11392]

501 Lejeune, Emilie. "Reminiscences of the French Opera
    in New Orleans. " Louisiana Historical Society Pub-
    lications, 9 (1916), 41-43. (1872)

502 Nolan, Paul T. "Espy Williams: New Orleans Play-
    wright. " Louisiana Library Association Bulletin, 21
    (Winter, 1958), 137-139. (1874-1908)

503 _____. "The Journal of a Young Southern Playwright,
    Espy Williams of New Orleans, 1874-1875. " Louisi-
    ana Studies, 1 (Fall, 1962), 30-50; (Winter, 1962),
    33-54.

504 Coleman, Marion Moore. "Modjeska and New Orleans. "
    Polish American Studies, 24 (January-June, 1967),
    1-14. (1879-1901)

505 O'Neal, Aaron Burwood. "History of the St. Charles
    Theatre of New Orleans, 1880-1888. " M. A. Lou-
    isiana State University, 1965.

506 Roden, Sally Ann. "History of the St. Charles Theatre
    of New Orleans Under the Management of David Bid-
    well, 1880-1888. " M. S. North Texas State Univer-
    sity, 1969.

507 Ross, Allan Sutphin. "The New Orleans Academy of
       Music Theatre, 1880-1887. " M. A. Louisiana State
       University, 1965.

508 Kendall, John Smith. "Sarah Bernhardt in New Orleans. "
       Louisiana Historical Quarterly, 26 (July, 1943), 770-
       782. (1880-)

509 Harrison, Shirley. "New Orleans: Greenwall vs. the
       Syndicate. " Players, 46 (April-May, 1971), 180-
       187. (1882)

510 Barello, Rudolph Valentino. "A History of the New Or-
       leans Academy of Music Theatre, 1887-1893. " M. A.
       Louisiana State University, 1967.

511 Lawlor, Jo Ann. "History of the St. Charles Theatre
       of New Orleans, 1888-1899. " M. A. Louisiana State
       University, 1966.

512 Head, Sadie Faye Edwards. "A Historical Study of the
       Tulane and Crescent Theatres of New Orleans, Lou-
       isiana, 1897-1937. " Ph. D. Louisiana State Univer-
       sity, 1963. 314 p. [64-05045]

       See also 1427.

OPELOUSAS

513 Dougherty, Edward B. "Presentational Entertainments
       in Opelousas, Louisiana, from 1886 through 1900. "
       M. A. Louisiana State University, 1953.

       See also 516, 517.

SHREVEPORT

514 Lindsey, Henry Carlton. "The History of the Theatre
       in Shreveport, Louisiana to 1900. " M. A. Louisiana
       State University, 1951. (1854-)

       See also 517.

THIBOUDAUX

       See 516, 517.

WASHINGTON

   See 517.

GENERAL

515   Bradford, Clinton William.   "The Non-Professional The-
      ater in Louisiana: A Survey of Organized and Mis-
      cellaneous Theatrical Activities from the Beginnings
      to 1900. "   Ph. D. Louisiana State University, 1951.
      x, 576 p.   (1810-)

516   Teague, Oran B. "The Professional Theater in Rural Loui-
      siana. "   M. A. Louisiana State University, 1952.   146 p.
      (Opelousas, Plaquemine, Thiboudaux) (1842-1885)

517   Parsons, Bill.   "The Debut of Adah Isaacs Menken. "
      Quarterly Journal of Speech, 46 (February, 1960),
      8-13.   (Alexandria, Houma, Opelousas, Shreveport,
      Thiboudaux, Washington) (1856-1857)

518   Dugdale, Mattie Wood.   "Travelers' Views of Louisiana
      before 1860. "   M. A. University of Texas, 1938.

519   Nolan, Paul T.   "The Case for Louisiana Drama. "
      Southwestern Louisiana Journal, 4 (January, 1960),
      35-42.

520   Sloane, Karen Williamson.   "Plays About Louisiana,
      1870-1915: A Checklist. "   Louisiana Studies, 8
      (Spring, 1969), 26-35.

521   Parsons, Billy Dean.   "The Contributions of James S.
      Charles to the Professional and Non-Professional
      Theatre in Louisiana. "   M. A. Louisiana State Uni-
      versity, 1958.

   See also 1421, 1426.

MAINE

BANGOR

522   Meinecke, Charlotte Drummond.   "Annals of the Drama

in Bangor, Maine, 1834-1882. " M. A. University of
Maine, 1941.

523 Thurston, Frederick Clark. "Annals of the Stage in
     Bangor, Maine, 1882-1900. " M. A. University of
     Maine, 1940.

PORTLAND

524 Moreland, James. "The Theatre in Portland in the
     Eighteenth Century. " New England Quarterly, 11
     (June, 1938), 331-342. (1792-1800)

525 _____ . "A History of the Theatre in Portland, 1794-
     1850. " M. A. University of Maine, 1934. 2 vols.
     (later updated to 1932)

526 _____ . The Theatre, a Picture History ... with
     Special Reference to the Theatre in Portland, Maine.
     Augusta, Maine, 1936.

527 Cail, Harold L. 'Famous American Theatres. " The-
     atre Arts, 40 (September, 1956), 69. (1897-1933)

MARYLAND

ANNAPOLIS

528 Ward, Kathryn Painter. "The First Professional The-
     ater in Maryland and Its Colonial Setting. " Mary-
     land Historical Magazine, 70 (Spring, 1975), 29-44.
     (1752)

529 Black, Mary Childs. "The Theatre in Colonial Annap-
     olis. " 1952. 139 p. (1752-1773)

530 Minto, (?). "Theatrical Performances during the Re-
     volution. " Magazine of American History, 6 (Jan-
     uary, 1881), 59. (1783)

531 Riley, Elihu Samuel. "The Ancient City": A History
     of Annapolis, in Maryland, 1649-1887. Annapolis:
     Annapolis Record Printing Office, 1887. pp. 146-148.

See also 536, 1407, 1408.

BALTIMORE

532 Shaffer, Virginia Mae. "The Theater in Baltimore
     (From Its Beginnings to 1786). " M. A. Johns Hop-
     kins University, 1926.   (1770-)

533 Ritchey, Robert David. "A History of the Baltimore
     Stage in the Eighteenth Century. " Ph. D. Louisiana
     State University, 1971.   373 p.   [72-03520] (1772-)

534 Bond, Chrystelle Trump. "A Chronicle of Dance in
     Baltimore, 1780-1814. " Dance Perspectives, 17
     (Summer, 1976), 3-49.

535 Ritchey, David. "The Maryland Company of Comedians. "
     Educational Theatre Journal, 24 (December, 1972),
     355-362.   (1781-1785)

536 Haims, Lynn. "First American Theatre Contracts:
     Wall and Lindsay's Maryland Company of Comedians,
     and the Annapolis, Fell's Point, and Baltimore The-
     atres, 1781-1783. " Theatre Survey, 17 (November,
     1976), 179-194.

537 "18th Century Theatre Bills of Baltimore and Annapolis. "
     Maryland History Notes, 12 (May, 1954), 1-2.   (1781-
     1782)

538 Ritchey, David. "Baltimore's Eighteenth Century French
     Theatre. " Southern Speech Communication Journal,
     38 (Winter, 1972), 164-167.   (1790-1796)

539 _____ . "The Baltimore Theatre and Yellow Fever
     Epidemic. " Maryland Historical Magazine, 67 (Fall,
     1972), 298-301.   (1793)

540 Stoddard, Richard. "Notes on John Joseph Holland, with
     a Design for the Baltimore Theatre, 1802. " Theatre
     Survey, 12 (May, 1971), 58-66.

541 Ritchey, David. "Columbia Garden: Baltimore's First
     Pleasure Garden. " Southern Speech Communication
     Journal, 39 (Spring, 1974), 241-247.   (1805-1807)

542 Howard, George W. The Monumental City: Its Past

History and Present Resources. Baltimore: J. D.
Ehlers & Co. , 1873. pp. 337-338. (1829-1866)

543 Zucker, Adolf E. "The History of the German Theater
in Baltimore. " Germanic Review, 18 (April, 1943),
123-135. (1853-1888)

544 Kuemmerle, Clyde V. "A History of Ford's Grand Opera House, Baltimore: From Its Origin in 1871 to
Its Demise in 1964. " M. A. University of Maryland,
1965.

545 Shepherd, Henry G. "Drama, Theater and Music. "
Baltimore: Its History and Its People. Ed. Clayton
Colman Hall. N. Y. : Lewis Historical Publishing
Co. , 1912. Vol. 1, pp. 651-655.

546 "Geschichte der Deutschen Buhne. " Baltimore: Seine
Vergangenheit und Gegenwart. Baltimore, Md. ,
1887. pp. 135-142.

See also 1408, 1413.

FELL'S POINT

See 536.

GENERAL

547 Palmer, John Williamson. "Manners and the Playhouse
in Old Maryland. " The Looker-On, November, 1896,
pp. 353-364. (1752-)

548 Heyl, Edgar. "Plays by Marylanders, 1870-1916. "
Maryland Historical Magazine, 62 (December, 1967),
438-447; 63 (March, 1968), 70-77; (June, 1968),
179-187; (December, 1968), 420-426; 64 (Spring,
1969), 74-77; (Winter, 1969), 412-419; 65 (Summer,
1970), 181-184; (Fall, 1970), 301-303; 67 (Spring,
1972), 71-83.

See also 1418.

MASSACHUSETTS

BOSTON

549 Woodruff, John Rowland. "The Theatrical Venture in
     Boston As Exemplified by the First Seasons of the
     Howard Athenaeum. " Ph. D. Cornell University,
     1949. 315 p. (1620-1848)

550 Reardon, William Robert. "The Tradition Behind Bos-
     tonian Censorship. " Educational Theatre Journal,
     7 (May, 1955), 97-101. (1620-1797)

551 Morse, William N. "Contributions to the History of the
     New England Stage in the Eighteenth Century, with
     Special Reference to Boston and Portsmouth. " Ph. D.
     Harvard University, 1936. 392 p. [Private manu-
     script on deposit; can be consulted only with written
     permission of the author or his heirs.] (1620-1789)

552 Reardon, William Robert. "Banned in Boston. A Study
     of Theatrical Censorship in Boston from 1630-1950. "
     Ph. D. Stanford University, 1952. 250 p. [00-05386]

553 Bonawitz, Dorothy Morgan. "The History of the Boston
     Stage from the Beginning to 1810. " Ph. D. Pennsyl-
     vania State University, 1936. 342 p. (1700-)

554 Clapp, William Warland. A Record of the Boston Stage.
     Boston and Cambridge: J. Munroe and Company,
     1853. 479 p. (1749-1850)

555 _____. "The Drama in Boston. " The Memorial
     History of Boston, Including Suffolk County, Mas-
     sachusetts, 1630-1880. Ed. Justin Winsor. Boston:
     Ticknor and Company, 1881. Vol. 4, pp. 358-382.

556 Hale, Philip. "A Boston Dramatic Critic of a Century
     Ago. " Proceedings of the Massachusetts Historical
     Society, 59 (1926), 312-324. (1750-1823)

557 Corbett, Alexander, Jr. "The Boston Theatre. " The
     Bostonian, 1 (October, 1894), 1-18. (1750-)

558 Vail, Robert W. G. "Boston's First Play. " Proceedings
     of the American Antiquarian Society, New Series, 49
     (October, 1939), 283-286. (1759)

559 Lees, C. Lowell. "First Nighters of Eighteenth Century
     America: IV. Boston ... The Oppositionalists. "
     Players Magazine, 13 (September-October, 1936),
     4-5, 14. (1759-)

560 Lansing, Marion Florence. "Historic Happenings on
     Boston Common: Pageants of Revolutionary Days. "
     New England Magazine, New Series, 42 (August,
     1910), 727-731. (1774)

561 Brown, Jared A. "The Theatre in Boston 1775-1776. "
     Players, 51 (February-March, 1976), 82-85.

562 Ford, Worthington Chauncey. "Prologue to Zara, 1776. "
     Massachusetts Historical Society Proceedings, 56
     (1923), 260-263.

563 Morison, Samuel Eliot. "Two 'Signers' on Salaries
     and the Stage, 1789. " Proceedings of the Massachu-
     setts Historical Society, 62 (1928-1929), 55-64.

564 Shaw, Robert Gould. Exhibition; Prints, Playbills, Ad-
     vertisements, and Autograph Letters to Illustrate
     the History of the Boston Stage From 1791 to 1825,
     From the Collection of Mr. Robert Gould Shaw,
     April 20 to April 25, 1914. Boston: Cockayne,
     1914. 41 p.

565 Michael, Mary Ruth. "A History of the Professional
     Theatre in Boston from the Beginning to 1816. "
     Ph. D. Radcliffe College, 1942. 3 vols. 1404 p.
     (1792-)

566 Ruff, Loren K. "Joseph Harper and Boston's Board
     Alley Theatre, 1792-1793. " Educational Theatre
     Journal, 26 (March, 1974), 45-52.

567 Fanger, Iris M. "Boston Goes to the Ballet, 1792-
     1797. " Dance Magazine, 50 (July, 1976), 47-49.

568 Gardiner, John. "Theatre: 1792. " Theatre Arts, 18
     (August, 1934), 621-622.

569 Toscan, Richard Eric. "The Organization and Operation
     of the Federal Street Theatre From 1793 to 1806. "
     Ph. D. University of Illinois Urbana, 1970. iv, 121 p.
     [71-05264]

570 Brown, Frank Chouteau. "The First Boston Theatre on
     Federal Street: Built 1793, Finally Discontinued
     1852, Charles Bulfinch, Architect. " Old-Time New
     England, 36 (July, 1945), 1-7.

571 Stoddard, Richard Foster. "A Reconstruction of Charles
     Bulfinch's First Federal Street Theatre, Boston. "
     Winterthur Portfolio, 6 (1970), 185-208.   (1793-1794)

572 _____ . "The Architecture and Technology of Boston
     Theatres, 1794-1854. " Ph. D. Yale University, 1971.
     iii, 281 p.   [71-31017]

573 Ball, William Thomas Winsborough. "The Old Federal
     Street Theatre. " Bostonian Society Publication, 8
     (1911), 41-92.   (1794-1852)

574 Alden, John Eliot. "A Season in Federal Street; J. B.
     Williamson and the Boston Theatre, 1796-1797. "
     American Antiquarian Society Proceedings, 65 (April,
     1955), 9-74.

575 Stoddard, Richard. "The Haymarket Theatre, Boston. "
     Educational Theatre Journal, 27 (March, 1975), 63-
     69.   (1796-1803)

576 _____ . "Aqueduct and Iron Curtain at the Federal
     Street Theatre, Boston. " Theatre Survey, 8 (No-
     vember, 1967), 106-111.   (1798-1835)

577 _____ . "Stock Scenery in 1798. " Theatre Survey,
     13 (November, 1972), 102-103.

578 Collins, Sherwood. "Boston's Political Theatre: The
     Eighteenth-Century Pope Day Pageants. " Educational
     Theatre Journal, 25 (December, 1973), 401-409.

579 Haley, Whitney Watson. "Robert Treat Paine, Jr. , and
     Early Theatrical Criticism in Boston. " M. A. Tufts
     University, 1958.

580 Blackall, C. H. "The Colonial Theatre and Building. "
     The American Architect, 72 (April 6, 1901), 11-12;

(April 27, 1901), 27-28; (May 11, 1901), 44-45;
(May, 18, 1901), 51-52; (June 1, 1901), 67-69.

581 Oliver, Peter. "The Boston Theatre, 1800. " Colonial
     Society of Massachusetts Publications, 34 (1943),
     554-570.

582 Gafford, Lucile. "The Boston Stage and the War of
     1812. " New England Quarterly, 7 (June, 1934), 327-
     335. (1812-1816)

583 Shaw, Robert Gould. Exhibition of Prints and Playbills
     to Illustrate the History of the Boston Stage (1825-
     1850): From the Collection of Mr. Robert Gould
     Shaw. May 3 to May 8, 1915. Boston: Cockayne,
     1915. 101 p.

584 Stoddard, Richard. "Isaiah Rogers' Tremont Theatre,
     Boston. " Antiques, 105 (June, 1974), 1314-1319.
     (1827-1843)

585 Fletcher, Edward Garland. "Charlotte Cushman's The-
     atrical Debut. " Studies in English, (1940), 166-175.
     University of Texas Publication No. 4026. (1835)

586 Kile, Sara Amanda. "John B. Wright's Staging at the
     National Theatre, Boston, 1836 to 1853. " M. A. Ohio
     State University, 1959.

587 McGlinchee, Claire. "The History of the First Decade
     of the Boston Museum. " Ph. D. Columbia University,
     1939. 370 p. (1841-1851)

588 _____. The First Decade of the Boston Museum.
     Boston: Bruce Humphries, Inc. , 1940. 370 p.
     (1841-1851)

589 Ticknor, Howard Malcom. "The Passing of the Boston
     Museum. " New England Magazine, 28 (June, 1903),
     378-396. (1841-)

590 Stebbins, Oliver B. "The Oldest Theatre Now in Bos-
     ton. " The Bostonian, 1 (November, 1894), 113-130.
     (1841-)

591 History of the Boston Museum. Boston, 1892. 35 p.
     (1843-1892)

592 Ryan, Kate. Old Boston Museum Days. Boston: Little,
     Brown, 1915. 264 p.

593 Mammen, Edward William. "The Old Stock Company
     School of Acting: A Study of the Boston Museum."
     Ph. D. Columbia University, 1945. 89 p.

594 _____. "The Old Stock Company: The Boston Mu-
     seum and Other 19th Century Theaters." More Books,
     19 (January, 1944), 3-18; (February, 1944), 49-63;
     (March, 1944), 100-107; (April, 1944), 132-149;
     (May, 1944), 176-195. (1843-1893)

595 _____. The Old Stock Company School of Acting: A
     Study of the Boston Museum. Boston: Trustees of
     the Public Library, 1945. 89 p.

596 Brayley, Arthur Wellington. "Wood's Boston Museum.
     What the Razing of an Old Landmark Disclosed."
     Bostonian, 2 (May, 1895), 125-130.

597 Woodruff, John Rowland. "America's Oldest Living
     Theatre-the Howard Athenaeum." Theatre Annual,
     8 (1950), 71-81. (1845-1950)

598 Stebbins, Oliver B. "A Famous Boston Amateur Dra-
     matic Club." The Bostonian, 2 (May, 1895), 131-140.
     (1847-1854)

599 Crawford, Mary Caroline. "The Old Boston Theatres
     and Their Stars." Romantic Days in Old Boston.
     Boston: Little, Brown & Co., 1910. pp. 238-280.

600 _____. "When Faneuil Hall Was a Playhouse"; "Early
     Boston Theatres and Their Stars." Old Boston Days
     and Ways. Boston: Little, Brown & Co., 1909.
     pp. 142-189, 419-457.

601 Eaton, W. O. "Stories of the Boston Stage By an Old
     Timer." 20 installments, Boston Commercial Bul-
     letin, 1876-1877.

602 Tompkins, Eugene, and Quincy Kilby. History of the
     Boston Theatre, 1854-1901. Boston and New York:
     Houghton, 1908. 550 p.

603 "The Boston Stage: Its History from 1854 to the Pres-
     ent Time." Boston Courier, 1874-1876.

604 Stebbins, Oliver B. "High Prices at Theatres. " Opera
Glass, 1 (September, 1894), 129-132. (1854-)

605 Stoddard, Roger E. "A Guide to 'Spencer's Boston Theatre', 1855-1862. " Proceedings of the American Antiquarian Society, 79 (April, 1969), 45-98.

606 Norcross, A. F. "A Child's Memory of the Boston Theatre. " Theatre, 43 (May, 1926), 37, 72. (1860's)

607 Young, James Harvey. "Anna Dickinson as Ann Boleyn. "
Emory University Quarterly, 5 (October, 1949), 163-
169. (1876)

608 Cahill, Thomas H. The Pocket Auditorium: Containing
Plans of Seats of All the Theaters and Halls of Boston. Boston: New England News Co. , 1878. 24 p.

609 The Theatrical Guide of the New England States. Boston,
1880-1882.

610 Grandgent, Charles A. "The Stage in Boston in the
Last Fifty Years. " Fifty Years of Boston. Boston,
1932. pp. 391-401.

611 Baker, George P. "From a Harvard Diary: Notes Made
in the Eighties. " Theatre Arts Monthly, 17 (July,
1933), 515-518. (1883-1885)

612 Stebbins, Oliver B. "Memorable Stage Hits. " Opera
Glass, 2 (January, 1895), 2-3. (1883-)

613 Skelton, Edward Oliver. Historical Review of the Boston Bijou Theatre, With the Original Casts of All
the Operas That Have Been Produced at the Bijou,
and With Photographs Illustrative of the Various Scenes
in Them. Boston: Edward O. Skelton, 1884. 72 p.

614 Wyman, Henry A. The Theatres: Summary of the
Dramatic Season of 1886-87, 1887-88. Boston, 1887,
1888. 2 vols.

615 Wingate, Charles Edgar Lewis. The Playgoers' Year-
Book, for 1888: Story of the Stage the Past Year
with Especial Reference to Boston. Boston: Stage
Publishing Co. , 1888. 87 p.

616 Pizer, Donald. "The Radical Drama in Boston 1889-1891. " New England Quarterly, 31 (September, 1958), 361-374.

617 Hatlan, Theodore W. " 'Margaret Fleming' and the Boston Independent Theatre. " Educational Theatre Journal, 8 (March, 1956), 17-21. (1891)

618 Pattee, Charles H. "Recollections of Old Play-Bills. " Arena, 4 (October, 1891), 604-614.

619 _____. "Recollections of Old Play-Bills. " The Bostonian, 2 (1895), 254-258.

620 "A Model Boston Theater. " The Dramatic Magazine, 2 (December, 1897-1898), 130-137. (1894-)

621 Morehouse, Ward. "Famous American Theatres. " Theatre Arts, 41 (August, 1957), 30. (1894-)

622 Thespian, pseud. Famous Playes and Their History: Being an Account of Some of the Most Celebrated Playes with Brief Biographical Notices of Famous Players, Original Casts, Copies of Old Play Bills, Anecdotes, etc. , with Special Reference to the Boston Stage. Boston, 1896.

623 Fluharty, George Watson. "Drama Activities in the Elizabeth Peabody House in Boston, --A History and Evaluation. " Ph. D. New York University, 1958. 315 p. [58-07616] (1896-1953)

624 French, Charles Elwell. Six Years of Drama at the Castle Square Theatre; With Portraits of the Members of the Company and Complete Programs of All Plays Produced, May 3, 1897-May 3, 1903. Boston: C. E. French, 1903. 406 p.

625 Heard, John R. Boston Theatres and Halls, With Historical Notes Past and Present; Chronology of Principle Dramatic and Musical Events. Boston: W. B. Jones, 1907. 32 p.

See also 1398, 1407, 1408, 1413.

CAMBRIDGE

626 Matthews, Albert. "Early Plays at Harvard. " Nation, 98 (March 19, 1914), 295. (1758-1781)

627 Flint, Martha M. "Dramatic Arts at Harvard University during the Nineteenth Century. " M. A. Columbia University, 1953. 61 p. (1758-)

628 R. , T. S. (Harvard's French Club.) The Theatre, 2 (February, 1902), 16-17. (1886-)

629 Garrison, Lloyd McKim. An Illustrated History of the Hasty Pudding Club Theatricals. Cambridge: Hasty Pudding Club, 1897, 1933. 270 p.

630 Orcutt, William Dana. "Clubs and Club Life at Harvard. " New England Magazine, New Series, 6 (March, 1892), 81-98. (1889-)

631 Hall, Richard W. "Recollections of the Cambridge Social Dramatic Club. " Cambridge Historical Society Publication, 38 (1959-1960), 51-67. (19th century)

632 Jones, Pauline. Cambridge Social Dramatic Club, 1890-1940; A Collection of Facts and Incidents Relating to the Founding and History of the Club. Cambridge, 1940. 18 p.

633 Cambridge Social Dramatic Club: Fiftieth Performance Given in Brattle Hall, February Fourteenth, 1903. Cambridge, 1903. 34 p. (1891-)

GLOUCESTER

634 Ellis, Melton. "Puritans and the Drama. " American Notes and Queries, 2 (July, 1942), 64. (1790)

JAMAICA PLAIN

635 Footlight Club, Jamaica Plain, Mass. A Scrap of Paper: Eliot Hall, Jamaica Plain, May 4-5, 1906. Cambridge: The Riverside Press, 1906. 52 p. (1877-1906)

LOWELL

636   Ordway, H. M.   "The Drama in Lowell, with a Short
        Sketch of the Life of Perez Fuller. "   Old Resident's
        Historical Association of Lowell, Contributions, 2
        (1880-1883), 268-288.   (1828-1866)

MEDFORD

637   Rockwell, Kenneth La Mar.   "Factors Contributing to
        the Rise and Growth of Dramatics in Tufts College:
        1852-1910. "   M. A. Tufts University, 1958.

MOUNT HOLYOKE

638   Wagner, Hilda Stahl.   "A History of Forms of Dramatic
        Expression in Mount Holyoke College, 1873-1950. "
        Ph. D. Teachers College, Columbia, 1953.   488 p.
        [00-06731]

NEWBURYPORT

639   Barriskill, James M.   "The Newburyport Theatre in the
        18th Century. "   Essex Institute Historical Collections,
        91 (July, 1955), 211-245.   (1774-1796)

640   _____ .   "The Newburyport Theatre in the 18th Cen-
        tury. "   Essex Institute Historical Collections, 91
        (October, 1955), 329-352.   (1797-1800)

641   _____ .   "Newburyport Theatre in the Federalist Pe-
        riod. "   Essex Institute Historical Collections, 93
        (January, 1957), 1-35.   (1800-1811)

642   _____ .   "Newburyport Theatre in the Early Nine-
        teenth Century. "   Essex Institute Historical Collec-
        tions, 93 (October, 1957), 279-314.   (1811-1825)

NORTHAMPTON

643   Hale, Philip.   "Musical and Theatrical Life in a New
        England Village in the Sixties. "   Massachusetts His-
        torical Society Proceedings, 56 (June, 1923), 335-343.

644   Wixander, Laurence E. , et al.   The Northampton Book:
        Chapters from 300 Years in the Life of a New Eng-
        land Town, 1654-1954.   Northampton, Mass. , ·1954.
        pp. 172-183.

645 Blake, Warren Barton. "America's Only Municipal Theatre." The Theatre, 20 (October, 1914), 166-170, 188. (1892-)

PITTSFIELD

646 Boltwood, Edward. The History of Pittsfield, Massachusetts from the Year 1876 to the Year 1916. Pittsfield: City of Pittsfield, 1916. Chapter 22.

SALEM

647 Hehr, Milton Gerald. "Musical Activities in Salem, Massachusetts, 1783-1823." Ph.D. Boston University, 1963. 441 p. [63-06574]

648 _____. "Theatrical Life in Salem, 1783-1823." Essex Institute Historical Collections, 100 (January, 1964), 3-37.

649 Ryan, Pat M., Jr. "The Old Salem Theatre." Essex Institute Historical Collections, 98 (October, 1962), 287-293. (1793-1830)

650 _____. "Young Hawthorne at the Salem Theatre." Essex Institute Historical Collections, 94 (July, 1958), 243-255. (1820-1830)

SPRINGFIELD

651 McEntire, Robert Miller. "Establishing Theater in a Provincial New England City: Springfield, Massachusetts, 1820-1900." Ph.D. Tufts University, 1971. 290 p. [72-30303]

WORCESTER

652 Paine, Nathaniel. "The Drama in Worcester." History of Worcester County, Mass. Ed. Duane Hamilton Hurd. Philadelphia: J.W. Lewis & Co., 1889. Vol. 2, pp. 1542-1546.

653 The Theatres and Public Halls of Worcester. 4th ed., Worcester, Mass., 1888. 20 p.

GENERAL

654 Little, Paul Judson. "Reactions to the Theatre: Vir-

ginia, Massachusetts, and Pennsylvania, 1665-1793. "
Ph. D. Syracuse University, 1969.   217 p. [70-12789]

MICHIGAN

ADRIAN

See 684.

ANN ARBOR

655 Behringer, Clara Marie.   "A History of the Theatre in
      Ann Arbor, Michigan, from Its Beginnings to 1904. "
      Ph. D. University of Michigan, Ann Arbor, 1950.   2
      vols.   xxii, 583 p.   [00-02379] (1824-)

656 Josenhans, M. Alma.   "Early Theatre in Ann Arbor,
      Michigan, 1835-1900. "   Washtenaw Impressions, 8
      (January, 1951), 1-11.

BAY CITY

657 Gore, John H.   "A History of Platform and Stage in Bay
      City, Michigan in the Nineteenth Century. "   Ph. D.
      Wayne State University, 1966.   2 vols.   v, 1042 p.
      [69-12010] (1864-1900)

BELDING

658 Wilson, Jack A.   "A History of the Belding Opera
      House, Belding, Michigan, from 1889-1915. "   M. A.
      Michigan State University, 1965.

CHEBOYGAN

659 Ridge, Patricia.   "A History of the Cheboygan Opera
      House, Cheboygan, Michigan, from 1891 to 1920. "
      M. A. Michigan State University, 1963.

COLDWATER

660 Gillespie, Carolyn L.   "A History of the Tibbits Opera

House, 1882-1904. " Ph. D. Kent State University,
1975. 303 p. [75-27810]

DETROIT

661 Josenhans, M. Alma. "The Theatre in Detroit, 1709-
1834. " Detroit Public Library News Bulletin, 9
(February, 1944), 5-8.

662 Brink, Alice Martin. "The Drama of Detroit from Its
Inception to 1870. With a Chronological Catalog of
Plays Presented in Detroit Theatres from 1840 to
1869. " M. A. Wayne State University, 1937. (1789-)

663 McDavitt, Elaine Elizabeth. "The Beginnings of Theatrical Activities in Detroit. " Michigan History, 31
(March, 1947), 35-47. (1815-1833)

664 Derse, J. E. "Entertainment in Early Detroit. " Michigan History Magazine, 30 (July-September, 1946),
504-507. (1816-1830)

665 McDavitt, Elaine Elizabeth. "A History of the Theatre
in Detroit, Michigan from Its Beginnings to 1862. "
Ph. D. University of Michigan, Ann Arbor, 1946.
viii, 556 p. (1833-)

666 Kistler, Mark O. "The German Theater in Detroit. "
Michigan History, 47 (December, 1963), 289-300.
(1850-1908)

667 Rudick, Lawrence William. "The Detroit Theatre Comes
of Age, 1862-1875. " Ph. D. Stanford University,
1971. x, 641 p. [71-23554]

668 Nobles, Milton. "Some Unwritten Stage History. " The
Theatre, 24 (July, 1916), 32. (1868)

669 Tutor, Richard Marlin. "The History of the Detroit
Opera House, 1869-1897. " Ph. D. Wayne State University, 1972. 2 vols. vi, 405 p. [73-12611]

670 Peterson, William Arthur. "A History of the Professional Theatre of Detroit, Michigan, September 13,
1875 to July 3, 1886. " Ph. D. Florida State University, 1959. 661 p. [59-03486]

671 Stark, George W. "Famous American Theatres. " Theatre Arts, 41 (May, 1957), 80. (1875-)

672 Josenhans, M. Alma. Chief Actors in Detroit, Michigan, 1875-1900. Detroit, 1956.

673 Spear, Richard D. "The Theatre in Detroit, 1885-1895,
as Revealed by the Dramatic Criticism of George P.
Goodale. " M. A. Wayne State University, 1954.

674 Aldridge, Henry Belden. "Live Musical and Theatrical
Presentations in Detroit Moving Picture Theatres:
1896-1930. " Ph. D. University of Michigan, Ann Arbor, 1973. xii, 314 p. [74-15656]

675 Hezlep, William E. "A History of the Detroit Opera
House, 1898-1931. " Ph. D. Wayne State University,
1973. v, 320 p. [73-31729]

676 Catlin, George Byron. "Early Detroit Theaters. " The
Story of Detroit. Detroit: The Detroit News, 1926.

EAST SAGINAW

677 Rydahl, Eugene Elvin. "A History of the Legitimate
Theatre in East Saginaw, Michigan, from 1860-1884. "
Ph. D. University of Iowa, 1958. 412 p. [58-05857]

FLINT

678 Sheridan, Charles Henry. "The History of Music Hall
Opera House, Flint, Michigan, 1883-1893. " M. A.
Wayne State University, 1951.

MARSHALL

See 684.

MASON

See 684.

MOUNT PLEASANT

679 Bush, Joan Donner. "The History of Dramatic Activities at Central Michigan College of Education from
1892 to 1950. " M. A. Michigan State University,
1951.

OXFORD

680 Bush, Karen E.   "The Oxford Opera House, Oxford,
        Michigan, in Its Hour: 1891-1914. " M. A. Michigan
        State University, 1966.

TRAVERSE CITY

681 Haines, Peggy A.   "The History of the City Opera House,
        Traverse City, Michigan, from 1891 until July of
        1897. " M. A. Eastern Michigan University, 1971.
        57 p.

YPSILANTI

682 Struck, James A.   "The History of Theatre at Eastern
        Michigan University, 1849 to 1959. " M. A. Eastern
        Michigan University, 1971.   81 p.

GENERAL

683 Dunbar, Willis F.   "The Opera House as a Social In-
        stitution in Michigan. " Michigan History Magazine,
        27 (October-December, 1943), 661-672.   (1870's)

684 Shanower, Donald Thomas.   "A Comparative and De-
        scriptive Study of Three Opera Houses in Southern
        Michigan, 1880-1900. " Ph. D. University of Michigan,
        Ann Arbor, 1959.   ix, 476 p.   [60-01793] (Adrian,
        Marshall, Mason)

MINNESOTA

DULUTH

685 Foreman, Larry M.   "A History of the Lyceum Thea-
        tre, Duluth, Minnesota, From 1891-1901. " Ph. D.
        University of Colorado, Boulder, 1977.   244 p.
        [77-24208]

MANKATO

686 Francis, Mark S.   "The Mankato Opera House: Music

on the Frontier, 1872-1885. " M. M. Mankato State
University, 1975.

MINNEAPOLIS

687 Edgar, Randolph. "Early Minneapolis Theatres. " Min-
     nesota History, 9 (March, 1928), 31-38. (1853-1894)

688 Woods, Donald Z. "A History of the Theatre in Min-
     neapolis, Minnesota, from Its Beginning to 1883. "
     Ph. D. University of Minnesota, 1950. 2 vols. 976 p.
     (1850's-)

689 _____. "Playhouse for Pioneers; the Story of the
     Pence Opera House. " Minnesota History, 33 (Winter,
     1952), 169-178. (1867-1952)

690 Appel, Livia. "Early Drama in Minneapolis. " Minne-
     sota History Bulletin, 5 (February, 1923), 43-45.
     (1867-)

691 Zalusky, Joseph. "Early Theatre ... or the History of
     Entertainment in Minneapolis. " Hennepin County His-
     tory, Fall, 1960, pp. 3-7.

692 Gee, Robert Frederick. "A History of the Theatre at
     the University of Minnesota from Its Beginning to
     1937. " M. A. University of Minnesota, 1949. (1873-)

693 Grossman, Audley Mitchell, Jr. "The Professional Le-
     gitimate Theatre in Minneapolis from 1890 to 1910. "
     Ph. D. University of Minnesota, 1957. 2 vols. vii,
     780 p. [00-23934]

694 Quinn, Germain. Fifty Years Back Stage, Being the
     Life Story of a Theatrical Stage Mechanic. Minne-
     apolis: Stage Publishing Co. , 1926. 204 p.

695 Atwater, Isaac, ed. History of the City of Minneapolis,
     Minnesota. New York: Munsell & Company, 1893.
     Chapters 13 and 26.

     See also 706, 1446.

NEW ULM

     See 706.

ROCHESTER

696 Beatty, J. Ted. "Down Memory Lane" and "The Metropolitan Theatre." Olmsted County Historical Society
News Bulletin, 8 (January, 1954), 3-6.

ST. ANTHONY

See 706.

ST. PAUL

697 Whiting, Frank M. "A History of the Theatre in St.
Paul, Minnesota, from Its Beginning to 1890." Ph.D.
University of Minnesota, 1941. 2 vols. vii, 926 p.
(1821-)

698 _____. "Theatrical Personalities of Old St. Paul."
Minnesota History, 23 (December, 1942), 305-315.
(1850's)

699 Rothfuss, Hermann E. "The Early German Theater in
Minnesota." Minnesota History, 32 (June, 1951),
100-105. (1857-1892)

700 Hemming, Sister Mary Ruth. "The History of the Grand
Opera House of St. Paul, Minnesota, from 1883-
1889." M.A. Catholic University of America, 1951.

701 Elzey, John Myles. "Professional Legitimate Theatre
in Saint Paul, Minnesota, From 1890-1918." Ph.D.
University of Minnesota, 1972. 2 vols. 667 p.
[73-01010]

702 McKee, Rose. "St. Paul Theaters 'Way Back When'...."
St. Paul Daily News, February 18, 1934, mag. sec.
1, 9.

See also 1446.

ST. PETER

703 Anderson, Evelyn C. "A History of the Theatre in St.
Peter, Minnesota, from Its Beginning to 1930."
M.A. University of Minnesota, 1946. (1855-)

GENERAL

704 Oaks, Harold Rasmus. "An Interpretative Study of the
     Effects of Some Upper Midwest Productions of Uncle
     Tom's Cabin as Reflected in Local Newspapers Be-
     tween 1852 and 1860. " Ph. D. University of Minne-
     sota, 1964. 177 p. [65-00139]

705 Rothfuss, Hermann E. "The German Theater in Minne-
     sota. " Ph. D. University of Minnesota, 1949. 119 p.

706 _____ . "The Early German Theater in Minnesota. "
     Minnesota History, 32 (September, 1951), 164-173.
     (Minneapolis, New Ulm, St. Anthony) (1858-1890)

707 _____ . "Criticism of the German-American Theater
     in Minnesota. " Germanic Review, 27 (April, 1952),
     124-130. (1858-1887)

708 _____ . "Plays for Pioneers: German Drama in
     Rural Minnesota. " Minnesota History, 34 (Summer,
     1955), 239-242. (1859-1888)

709 _____ . "Theodore Steidle, German Theater Pioneer. "
     American German Review, 17 (February, 1951), 17-
     19, 33. (1861-1868)

710 Jensen, Andrew F. "Two Decades of Trouping in Minne-
     sota, 1865-1885. " Minnesota History, 28 (June,
     1947), 97-119.

711 DuBois, Cornelia Andrews. "Operatic Pioneers: The
     Story of the Andrews Family. " Minnesota History,
     33 (Winter, 1953), 317-325. (1875-1901)

712 Sherman, John K. "Music and Theatre in Minnesota
     History. " A History of the Arts in Minnesota. Ed.
     William Van O'Connor. Minneapolis: University of
     Minnesota Press, 1958. Sec. 1, pp. 3-63.

713 Brings, Lawrence Martin. Minnesota Heritage. Min-
     neapolis: T. S. Denison, 1960. pp. 272-284.

MISSISSIPPI

JACKSON

714 McKee, Edna Hollingsworth. "History of Theatrical Entertainment in Jackson, Mississippi, from August 1839 to April 1860." M.S. Florida State University, 1959. 62 p.

715 Stevens, Katherine Bell. "Theatrical Entertainment in Jackson, Mississippi, 1890-1900." M.A. University of Mississippi, 1951.

716 Hollister, Katherine Stevens. "The Theatre in Jackson, 1890-1910." Journal of Mississippi History, 17 (April, 1955), 127-134.

717 McCain, William David. The Story of Jackson: A History of the Capital of Mississippi, 1821-1951. Jackson, Miss.: J.F. Hyer Publishing Co., 1953. Vol. 1, pp. 118-131.

NATCHEZ

718 Hamil, Linda Virginia. "A Study of Theatrical Activity in Natchez, Mississippi from 1800-1840." M.A. University of Mississippi, 1976.

719 Free, Joseph Miller. "The Ante-Bellum Theatre of the Old Natchez Region." Journal of Mississippi History, 5 (January, 1943), 14-27. (1806-1840)

720 Hamilton, William Baskerville. "American Beginnings in the Old Southwest: The Mississippi Phase." Ph.D. Duke University, 1938. 4 parts. (Only Part 2 on drama; printed in 721)

721 _____. "The Theatre of the Old Southwest; The First Decade at Natchez." American Literature, 12 (January, 1941), 471-485. (1808-1818)

722 Gates, William Bryan. "The Theatre in Natchez." Journal of Mississippi History, 3 (April, 1941), 71-129. (1809-1850)

See also 723, 724.

VICKSBURG

See 723, 724.

GENERAL

723 Free, Joseph Miller. "Studies in American Theatre
     History: The Theatre of Southwestern Mississippi to
     1840. " Ph. D. University of Iowa, 1941. 2 vols.
     735 p. (1806-)

724 Gates, William Bryan. "Performances of Shakespeare
     in Ante-Bellum Mississippi. " Journal of Mississippi
     History, 5 (January, 1943), 28-37. (Natchez, Vicks-
     burg) (1814-1860)

725 Finley, Katherine P. , and Paul T. Nolan. "Mississippi
     Drama Between Wars, 1870-1916: A Checklist and
     an Argument. " Journal of Mississippi History, 26
     (August, 1964), 219-228; (November, 1964), 299-306.

     See also 1421.

MISSOURI

BOONVILLE

726 Swanson, Alice Holbrook. "A History of Thespian Hall
     in Boonville, Missouri: 1855-1914. " M. A. Memphis
     State University, 1972.

727 A Brief History of Thespian Hall, Boonville, Missouri.
     Boonville, Missouri: Thespian Hall Preservation
     Committee, 1937. 16 p. (1857-)

728 Melton, Elston Joseph. The First Hundred Years: With
     a Chapter on Movies and Home Talents, by Opal Hol-
     lomon Melton. Boonville: Missourian Publications,
     1957. 56 p.

729 "Boonville Hopes to See Old Thespian Hall Accepted as
     a National Shrine. " Missouri Historical Review, 31
     (April, 1937), 354-356. (1857)

     See also 785, 788.

CAPE GIRARDEAU

730 Jones, Martha Howard. "Show Business in the Boot-
     heel-A History of the Performing Arts in Cape Gir-
     ardeau, Missouri, 1868-1963. " M. S. Southern Illi-
     nois University, Carbondale, 1963.

COLUMBIA

     See 335, 785.

FAYETTE

     See 785.

HANNIBAL

     See 785, 788.

HERMANN

     See 788.

JEFFERSON CITY

     See 335, 785, 788.

JOPLIN

731 "Joplin's First Theatre. " Missouri Historical Review,
     21 (October, 1926), 141-142. (1875)

KANSAS CITY

732 Rietz, Louise Jean. "History of the Theatre of Kansas
     City, Missouri, from the Beginnings until 1900. "
     Ph. D. University of Iowa, 1939. 3 vols. 1003 p.
     (1858-)

733 Briggs, Harold E. , and Ernestine Bennett Briggs. "The
     Theatre in Early Kansas City. " Mid-America, 32
     (April, 1950), 89-103. (1858-1870)

734 Peck, Phoebe. "The Theater in Kansas City. " M. A.
     University of Missouri, Kansas City, 1940. (1858-
     1906)

735 Mackey, Alice. "A History of the Coates Opera House,
     Kansas City, Missouri, 1870-1901. " M. A. Central
     Missouri State University, 1963.

736 Taylor, W. Ellard, Jr. "A Survey of Selected Profes-
     sional Theatre Buildings, Kansas City, Missouri,
     1870-1902. " M. A. Central Missouri State Univer-
     sity, 1968.

737 Coiner, Miles W. , Jr. "The Grand Opera House and
     the Golden Age of the Legitimate Theater in Kansas
     City. " Missouri Historical Review, 67 (April, 1973),
     407-423.   (1891-)

738 Latchaw, David A. "The Enchanted Years of the Stage--
     Recollections of the Stage in Kansas City in Its Early
     Days and of Its Most Distinctive Actors. " (series of
     60 articles) Kansas City Star, March 23 to June 23,
     1935.

     See also 788.

LEXINGTON

     See 785, 788.

PALMYRA

     See 785.

ST. JOSEPH

739 "St. Joseph Thespian Society. " Missouri Historical Re-
     view, 27 (January, 1933), 172.   (1845)

740 Karasz, Lawrence J. "A History of Legitimate Theatre
     in St. Joseph, Missouri, 1865-1900. " M. A. South-
     west Missouri State University, 1972.

741 Merrill, Patricia Ellene. "A History of the Tootle Op-
     era House, St. Joseph, Missouri. " M. A. University
     of Missouri, Kansas City, 1973. (1872-1925)

742 Howe, Edgar Watson. "Ed Howe on Sarah Bernhardt. "
     Kansas Historical Quarterly, 18 (May, 1950), 209-
     212. (1881)

     See also 785.

ST. LOUIS

743 Carson, William Glasgow Bruce. The Theatre on the
     Frontier: The Early Years of the St. Louis Stage.
     Chicago: University of Chicago Press, 1932. 361 p.
     (1814-1839)

744 _____. "The Beginnings of the Theatre in St. Louis. "
     Missouri Historical Society Collections, 5 (February,
     1928), 129-165. (1815-1820)

745 Shoemaker, Floyd C. "The Lure of the Footlights and
     Professional Acting Drew Missourians to Frontier
     Theater. " Missouri Historical Review, 46 (April,
     1952), 252-254. (1818-1859)

746 Mayer, Harold Francis. "Materials for a History of
     Dramatics in Saint Louis University from 1818 to
     1900. " M. A. Saint Louis University, 1938.

747 Hesse, Richard Michel. "Aspects of the Early St. Lou-
     is Stage. " M. A. Washington University, 1950.
     (1819-1851)

748 "The Summer Beer Gardens of St. Louis. " Missouri
     Historical Society Bulletin, 9 (July, 1953), 391-395.
     (1823-1903)

749 Moss, James E. "Dramatic Criticism in Frontier St.
     Louis 1835-1838. " Missouri Historical Review, 58
     (January, 1964), 191-216.

750 Brown, Lawrence Robert, "Frontier Dramatic Criticism,
     St. Louis, 1835-1839. " M. S. University of Wiscon-
     sin, Madison, 1949.

751 Carson, William G. B. "Sol Smith and Theatre Folk,
     1836-1865. " Missouri Historical Society Glimpses
     of the Past, 5 (1938), 99-136.

752 _____. "Night Life in St. Louis a Century Ago. "
Missouri Historical Society Bulletin, 1 (April, 1945),
3-9; 2 (October, 1945), 3-10. (1837-1844)

753 _____, ed. "The Diary of Matt Field, St. Louis,
April 2-May 16, 1839. " Missouri Historical Society
Bulletin, 5 (January, 1949), 91-108; (April, 1949),
157-184.

754 _____. Managers in Distress: The St. Louis Stage,
1840-1844. St. Louis: Historical Documents Foun-
dation, 1949. 329 p.

755 Waldemar and Buechel. Das Deutsche Theater in St.
Louis, 1842-1892. St. Louis, 1892.

756 Grisvard, Larry Eugene. "The Final Years: The Lud-
low and Smith Theatrical Firms in St. Louis, 1845-
1851. " Ph. D. Ohio State University, 1965. x,
307 p. [66-06261]

757 Blackburn, Margaret. "The Stage in St. Louis, Missouri after 1850. " M. A. University of Iowa, 1927.
(1850-1860)

758 Wilkinson, Alfred Oliver. "The St. Louis Dramatic
Seasons of 1850 and 1851. " M. A. Washington University, 1938.

759 Krone, Charles A. "Recollections of an Old Actor. "
Missouri Historical Collections, 2 (1906), 25-43; 3
(January, 1908), 53-70; (April, 1908), 170-182; 3
(1911), 275-306, 423-436; 4 (1912), 104-120; 4 (1913),
209-233; 4 (1914), 423-463. (1850's)

760 Herbstruth, Grant M. "Benedict Debar and the Grand
Opera House in St. Louis, Missouri, from 1855 to
1879. " Ph. D. University of Iowa, 1954. 2 vols.
1084 p. [00-09580]

761 Barbee, Bud. "St. Louis Drama in 1861 and 1862. "
M. A. Washington University, 1949.

762 Wilkinson, Colleen Mae. "A History of the Theatre in
St. Louis, 1865-1866. " M. A. Baylor University,
1954.

763 Johnson, Theodore Clark. "A History of the First Olym-
     pic Theatre of St. Louis, Missouri, from 1866-
     1879." Ph.D. University of Iowa, 1958.   343 p.
     [58-02970]

764 David, John Russell. "The Genesis of the Variety The-
     atre: The Black Crook Comes to Saint Louis." Mis-
     souri Historical Review, 64 (January, 1970), 133-149.
     (1867)

765 "Dramatic History of St. Louis." St. Louis Home Jour-
     nal, January 26; February 2, 9, 16, 23; March 1, 8,
     1868.

766 Hollingsworth, Gerelyn. "Legitimate Theater in St.
     Louis, 1870-1879." Missouri Historical Review, 69
     (April, 1975), 260-281.

767 Thompson, Isabel Cecilia. "Amateur Theatricals in St.
     Louis, Missouri, 1875-1890." Ph.D. University of
     Iowa, 1954.   2 vols.   596 p.   [00-09595]

768 Carson, William G.B. "Under the Calcium Lights:
     Actors Take to the Road, 1875-1877." Missouri His-
     torical Society Bulletin, 12 (July, 1956), 333-357.

769 Ryan, Pat M. "Wild Apaches in the Effete East: A
     Theatrical Adventure of John P. Clum." Theatre
     Survey, 6 (November, 1965), 147-156. (1876)

770 Hammack, James Alan. "Pope's Theatre and St. Louis
     Theatrical History, 1879-1895." Ph.D. University
     of Iowa, 1954.   2 vols.   446 p.   [00-09576]

771 Callahan, John Martin. "A History of the Second Olym-
     pic Theatre of Saint Louis, Missouri, 1882-1916."
     Ph.D. Kent State University, 1974.   549 p.   [75-
     11984]

772 _____. "A History of the Second Olympic Theatre
     of St. Louis, 1882-1916: The Norton Years." Mis-
     souri Historical Society Bulletin, 31 (July, 1975),
     231-252.   (1882-1889)

773 _____. "A History of the Second Olympic Theatre
     of St. Louis, 1882-1916: The Pat Short Years."
     Missouri Historical Society Bulletin, 32 (October,
     1975), 3-25.   (1889-1916)

774 Nolle, Alfred Henry. "The German Drama on the St.
     Louis Stage. " Ph. D. University of Pennsylvania,
     1915.   83 p.

775 _____ . "The German Drama on the St. Louis Stage. "
     German American Annals, 15 (January-May, 1917),
     28-65, 73-112.

776 _____ . The German Drama on the St. Louis Stage.
     Philadelphia: University of Pennsylvania Press,
     1917.   83 p. (Americana Germanica, No. 32)

777 Scharf, John Thomas. History of Saint Louis City and
     County, From The Earliest Periods to The Present
     Day. Philadelphia: L. H. Everts & Co. , 1883. Vol.
     1, pp. 959-988.

778 Hyde, William, and Howard L. Conard, eds. Encyclo-
     pedia of the History of St. Louis: A Compendium of
     History and Biography for Ready Reference. New
     York: The Southern History Company, 1899. Vol.
     4, pp. 2251-2261.

779 Stevens, Walter B. St. Louis the Fourth City, 1764-
     1909. St. Louis, 1909. Vol. 1, pp. 951-955.

     See also 335, 932.

SPRINGFIELD

780 Lampe, Michael. "Legitimate Theatre in Springfield,
     Missouri: 1840 to 1900. " M. A. Southwest Missouri
     State University, 1970.

WASHINGTON

     See 788.

GENERAL

781 Jacobs, Elijah L. "First Play Published in Missouri. "
     Missouri Historical Review, 45 (October, 1950),
     108-109. (1821)

782 Bowen, Elbert Russell. "Amusements and Entertain-
     ments in Early Missouri. " Missouri Historical Re-
     view, 47 (July, 1953), 307-317. (1821-1860)

783 _____. "Negro Minstrels in Early Rural Missouri. "
Missouri Historical Review, 47 (January, 1953), 103-
109. (1830-1860)

784 _____. "A Study of Theatrical Entertainment in Rural
Missouri before the Civil War. " Ph. D. University
of Missouri, Columbia, 1950. 2 vols. 557 p.
[00-01674] (1832-1861)

785 _____. "Thespian Societies in Rural Missouri. "
Missouri Historical Society Bulletin, 14 (July, 1958),
331-356. (Boonville, Columbia, Fayette, Hannibal,
Jefferson City, Lexington, Palmyra, St. Joseph)
(1832-1860)

786 _____. Theatrical Entertainments in Rural Missouri
before the Civil War. Columbia: University of Missouri Press, 1959. 141 p. University of Missouri
Studies, No. 32. (1837-1861)

787 _____. "The Circus in Early Rural Missouri. " Missouri Historical Review, 47 (October, 1952), 1-17.
(1838-1861)

788 _____. "The German Theatre of Early Rural Missouri. " Missouri Historical Review, 46 (January,
1952), 157-161. (Boonville, Hannibal, Hermann,
Jefferson City, Kansas City, Lexington, Washington)
(1843-1860)

789 "Melodies and Soft Shoes in Black-face. " Missouri Historical Review, 38 (January, 1944), 192-195. (1856-
1900)

790 West, William Francis, Jr. "The Legitimate Theatre
in Rural Missouri From the Beginning of the Civil
War Through 1872. " Ph. D. University of Missouri,
Columbia, 1964. 432 p. [64-13312]

791 Gilmore, Robert Karl. "Theatrical Elements in Folk
Entertainments in the Missouri Ozarks, 1885-1910. "
Ph. D. University of Minnesota, 1961. 290 p. [63-
01251]

792 McDermott, John Francis. "Culture and the Missouri
Frontier. " Missouri Historical Review, 50 (July,
1956), 355-370.

MONTANA

BILLINGS

See 800.

BOZEMAN

793 Jacobsen, Bruce Carl. "A Historical Study of the
    Bozeman, Montana Opera House. " Ph. D. Univer-
    sity of Minnesota, 1969. v, 222 p. [69-20089]
    (1890-1920)

794 DeHaas, John N. , and Bernice W. DeHaas. "Footlights
    and Fire Engines: Bozeman's City Hall-Opera House. "
    Montana: The Magazine of Western History, 17
    (October, 1967), 28-43. (1890-1927)

    See also 800.

BUTTE

795 Clark, Archie L. "John Maguire: Butte's 'Belasco. '"
    The Montana Magazine of History, 2 (January, 1952),
    33-40. (1875-1902)

    See also 800.

FORT BENTON

See 1447.

FORT SHAW

796 Chowen, Agnes B. "Theatricals at Fort Shaw in 1874-
    1875. " The Frontier, 12 (May, 1932), 303-308.

GREAT FALLS

See 800.

HELENA

See 800, 1452, 1457.

MILES CITY

See 1447.

MISSOULA

797 Coleman, Rufus A. , ed. "Daniel E. Bandmann, 1840-
1905. Shakespearean Stockman. " Montana Magazine
of History, 4 (Autumn, 1954), 29-43. (1884)

798 Partoll, Albert J. "Bandmann's Greatest Triumph. "
Montana Magazine of History, 5 (Spring, 1955), 29-
30.

See also 800.

VIRGINIA CITY

See 800, 1457.

GENERAL

799 Cochran, Alice. "The Gold Dust Trail: Jack Langrishe's Mining Town Theaters. " Montana: The Magazine of Western History, 20 (April, 1970), 58-69.
(1859-1885)

800 Brown, Firman Hewitt, Jr. "A History of Theater in
Montana. " Ph. D. University of Wisconsin, Madison,
1963. 2 vols. 665 p. [63-05735] (Billings, Bozeman, Butte, Great Falls, Helena, Missoula, Virginia
City) (1860's-)

801 Porter, Esther. "A Compilation of Materials for a
Study of the Early Theatres of Montana (1864-1880). "
M. A. University of Montana, 1938.

802 Nolan, Paul T. Montana Drama before World War I:
The Neglected Mine. np, nd.

803 Clark, Archie L. "The Montana Theatre in Stage Coach
and Steamboat Days. " A History of Montana. Ed.
Merrill Burlingame and J. Ross Toole. Helena,
Montana, 1957. Vol. 2, pp. 291-314.

See also 1456.

NEBRASKA

FREMONT

804 Schanke, Robert Anders. "Fremont's Love Opera House."
     Nebraska History, 55 (Summer, 1974), 221-253.
     (1888-1917)

805 _____ . "History of Speech and Drama at Midland
     College." M. A. University of Nebraska, Lincoln,
     1963.

LINCOLN

806 Ryan, Pat M. "Hallo's Opera House: Pioneer Theatre
     of Lincoln, Nebraska." Nebraska History, 45 (De-
     cember, 1964), 323-330. (1873-1902)

807 Gossage, Forest Donald. "A History of the Funke Opera
     House in Lincoln, Nebraska, 1884-1902." M. A. Uni-
     versity of Nebraska, Lincoln, 1961.

808 Hayes, Arthur Bradley, and Sam D. Cox. History of
     the City of Lincoln, Nebraska. Lincoln: State Jour-
     nal Company, 1889. Chapter 24.

809 Walton, James Harmon. "A History of Professional
     Theater at 'The Oliver' in Lincoln, Nebraska (1897-
     1918)." M. A. University of Nebraska, Lincoln,
     1956.

OMAHA

810 Harper, Robert D. "Theatrical Entertainment in Early
     Omaha." Nebraska History Magazine, 36 (June,
     1955), 93-104. (1857-1867)

811 Nobles, Milton. "Some Unwritten Stage History." The
     Theatre, 24 (July, 1916), 31. (1867-1868)

812 Fanders, Reuben. "History of the Boyd Theatre in
     Omaha, Nebraska. " M.A. University of Nebraska,
     Lincoln, 1963.

813 Deahl, William E. , Jr. "Nebraska's Unique Contri-
     bution to the Entertainment World. " Nebraska His-
     tory, 49 (Autumn, 1968), 283-297. (1883)

814 Savage, James Woodruff, and John T. Bell. History of
     the City of Omaha, Nebraska. N. Y. & Chicago:
     Munsell & Company, 1894. pp. 303-307.

815 Sorenson, Alfred. The Story of Omaha. 3rd ed. Oma-
     ha, 1923. Chapter 26.

816 Fanders, R. H. "When Omaha Had Its Golden Age of
     Theater. " Sunday World-Herald Magazine, October 6,
     1963, pp. 6-7.

GENERAL

817 Harper, Charles Harold. "The Dramatic Criticism of
     Willa Cather from 1893 to 1900. " M. A. University
     of Nebraska, Lincoln, 1967.

NEVADA

CARSON

818 Davis, Mrs. Sam P. "Early Theatrical Attractions in
     Carson. " Nevada State Historical Society Papers,
     4 (1923-1924), 201-212. (1866-1883)

VIRGINIA CITY

819 Watson, Margaret G. "History of the Theatre of Vir-
     ginia City, Nevada, from 1849-1865. " M. A. Uni-
     versity of Nevada, Reno, 1940. 215 p.

820 Miller, William Charles. "An Historical Study of The-
     atrical Entertainment in Virginia City, Nevada; or
     Bonanza and Borasca Theatres on the Comstock

(1860-1875). " Ph. D. University of Southern California, 1947. 2 vols. 656 p.

821 Demarest, Michael. "Opera on the Comstock Lode. "
Opera and Concert, 14 (October, 1949), 20-21.
(1860-1940)

822 Soldo, Betty Lougaris. "The Feminine Favorites of the
Virginia City Stage: 1865-1880. " M. A. California
State University, Fullerton, 1975. 94 p. [M-6741]

823 Nobles, Milton. "Some Unwritten Stage History. " The
Theatre, 24 (August, 1916), 79, 81, 94. (1870)

824 Crawford, Robert A. "History and Description of Piper's
Opera House, Virginia City, Nevada. " M. A. University of California, Los Angeles, 1950.

825 Cole, Wendell. "Piper's Opera House. " Western
Speech, 25 (Winter, 1961), 17-20. (1885-)

826 Hillyer, Katherine Custis, and Katherine Best. The
Amazing Story of Piper's Opera House in Virginia
City, Nevada. Virginia City, Nevada: Enterprise
Press, 1953. 23 p.

See also 79, 1453.

GENERAL

827 Semenza, Edwin S. "The History of the Professional
Theatre in the State of Nevada. " M. A. University
of Southern California, 1934. 115 p.

828 Ausburn, Lynna Joyce. "Highlights of the Theatre of
the West: Its Beginnings and Its Development on the
Mining Frontiers of California and Nevada. " M. A.
University of Tulsa, 1970. 148 p. (1849-1860's)

829 Watson, Margaret G. Silver Theatre: Amusements on
the Mining Frontier in Early Nevada, 1850 to 1864.
Glendale, California: Arthur H. Clark Co. , 1964.
387 p.

830 Ryan, Patrick M. , Jr. 'Mark Twain: Frontier Theatre Critic. " Arizona Quarterly, 16 (Summer, 1960),
197-209. (1863-1866)

831   Ericson, Robert Edward.   "Touring Entertainment in
        Nevada During the Peak Years of the Mining Boom,
        1876-1878. "   Ph. D. University of Oregon, 1970.   x,
        498 p. [71-01307]

      See also 1451.

NEW HAMPSHIRE

HANOVER

832   Rugg, Harold G.   "The Dartmouth Plays, 1779-1782. "
        Theatre Annual, 1 (1942), 55-69.

MANCHESTER

833   Hewitt, David D.   "A History of the Theater in Man-
        chester, N. H. " Dartmouth Senior English Thesis,
        1948.

PORTSMOUTH

834   Morse, William N.   "Contributions to the History of
        the New England Stage in the Eighteenth Century,
        with Special Reference to Boston and Portsmouth. "
        Ph. D. Harvard University, 1936.   392 p. [Private
        manuscript on deposit; can be consulted only with
        written permission of author or his heirs.] (1620-
        1789)

835   "Attempt to Establish a Play-house in New Hampshire,
        1762. " New Hampshire Historical Society Collec-
        tions, 5 (1837), 247-250.

      See also 1408.

NEW JERSEY

NEW BRUNSWICK

836 Coad, Oral Sumner. "The First Century of the New
     Brunswick Stage. " Journal of the Rutgers University
     Library, 5 (December, 1941), 15-36; (June, 1942),
     78-89; 6 (June, 1943), 52-57. (1783-1873)

837 _____. "The Masonic Hall Opera House: A Further
     Chapter in New Brunswick's Stage History. " Journal
     of the Rutgers University Library, 28 (June, 1965),
     1-14; 29 (December, 1965), 13-25. (1873-1896)

838 "Queens Players to Give Brother Rat. " Centre Aisle,
     3 (March 12, 1941), 1, 2, 4. (1888-)

NEWARK

839 Moore, Lester Lee. "A History of the Professional
     Theatre in Newark, New Jersey, from 1847-1867. "
     Ed. D. Teachers College, Columbia, 1966. 172 p.
     [67-06530]

840 _____. Outside Broadway: A History of the Pro-
     fessional Theater in Newark, New Jersey from the
     Beginning to 1867. Metuchen, N. J. : Scarecrow
     Press, 1970. 182 p. (1847-)

841 Hipp, Edward S. "Theaters Flourished in '80s. " New-
     ark Sunday News, September 21, 1958.

PRINCETON

842 Borgers, Edward William. "A History of Dramatic Pro-
     duction in Princeton, New Jersey. " Ph. D. New York
     University, 1950. 492 p. [00-01920] (1685-1948)

843 McAneny, Herbert. "Some Notes on Princeton Amuse-
     ments, Civil War to 1887. " Princeton University
     Library Chronicle, 4 (November, 1942), 10-29.

NEW MEXICO

ALBUQUERQUE

See 861.

LAS CRUCES

See 861.

ROSWELL

See 861.

SANTA FE

844 Woodward, Dorothy. "First Theater in English in New
        Mexico. " Eds. William Minor Dabney and Josiah
        Cox Russell. Dargan Historical Essays. Albuquer-
        que: University of New Mexico Press, 1952. pp.
        65-76. (1846)

845 Gartner, David. "A Detailed History of the Theatre in
        Santa Fe, New Mexico, 1847-1881, Containing, in
        Addition, an Outline of the Theatrical Activities in
        This City from 1881-1891. " M. A. Washington Uni-
        versity, 1951.

        See also 850, 861.

GENERAL

846 Austin, Mary. "Native Drama in Our Southwest. " Na-
        tion, 124 (April 20, 1927), 437-438, 440. (1595-)

847 McCrossan, Sister Joseph Marie. "The Role of the
        Church and the Folk in the Development of the Early
        Drama in New Mexico. " Ph. D. University of Penn-
        sylvania, 1945. 258 p.

848 _____ . The Role of the Church and the Folk in the
        Development of the Early Drama in New Mexico.
        Philadelphia: Dolphin Press, 1948. 172 p. (1598-
        1948)

849 Martin, Charles Basil. "The Survivals of Medieval Re-
     ligious Drama in New Mexico. " Ph. D. University of
     Missouri, Columbia, 1959.

850 "The First Community Theater and Playwright in the
     United States. " El Palacio, 16 (March 15, 1924),
     83-87. (New Mexico, Texas) (1598)

851 Johnston, Winifred. "Entertainments of the Spanish Ex-
     plorers. " Chronicle of Oklahoma, 8 (March, 1930),
     89-93. (1598)

852 _____. "Early Theatre in the Spanish Borderlands. "
     Mid-America, 13 (October, 1930), 121-131. (1598-)

853 Englekirk, John E. "Notes on the Repertoire of the
     New Mexican Spanish Folktheater. " Southern Folk-
     lore Quarterly, 4 (December, 1940), 227-237. (1598-)

854 Tarver, Katharine Feild. "Los Pastores. " M.A. South-
     western University, 1926. (Thesis at Our Lady of
     the Lake University, San Antonio)

855 Munro, Edwin C. "The Nativity Plays of New Mexico. "
     M.A. University of New Mexico, 1940. 87 p.

856 Campa, Arthur Leon. "Religious Spanish Folk-Drama
     in New Mexico. " New Mexico Quarterly, 2 (Febru-
     ary, 1932), 3-13.

857 _____. "Spanish Religious Folktheatre in the South-
     west (First Cycle). " University of New Mexico Bul-
     letin, Language Series, 5, No. 1 (1934), 5-16.

858 _____. "Spanish Religious Folktheatre in the South-
     west (Second Cycle). " University of New Mexico
     Bulletin, Language Series, 5, No. 2, (1934), 5-157.

859 _____. "The New Mexican Spanish Folktheater. "
     Southern Folklore Quarterly, 5 (June, 1941), 127-
     131.

860 Clum, John P. "Apaches as Thespians in 1876. " New
     Mexico Historical Review, 6 (January, 1931), 76-99.

861 Vineyard, Hazel. "Trails of the Trouper; A Historical
     Study of the Theater in New Mexico from 1880 to

1910. "   M. A. University of New Mexico, 1942.   110 p.
(Albuquerque, Las Cruces, Roswell, Santa Fe)

NEW YORK

ALBANY

862 Leonard, James Marshall. "The Letters of William
     Duffy, Albany Theatre Manager, 1830-1835. "   Ph. D.
     Cornell University, 1971.   265 p.   [71-17649]
     (1757-1835)

863 Phelps, Henry Pitt. Players of a Century: A Record
     of the Albany Stage. Albany: J. McDonough, 1880.
     424 p. (1760-1880)

864 Kime, Wayne R. "An Actor Among the Albanians: Two
     Rediscovered Sketches of Albany by Washington Ir-
     ving. " New York History, 56 (October, 1975), 409-
     425. (1803)

865 Kellerhouse, Muriel Arline. "The Green Street Theatre,
     Albany, New York Under the Management of John
     Bernard, 1813-1816. "   Ph. D. Indiana University,
     1973.   211 p.   [73-19740]

866 Stone, Henry Dickinson. Personal Recollections of the
     Drama; Or, Theatrical Reminiscences, Embracing
     Sketches of Prominent Actors and Actresses.   Al-
     bany: C. Van Benthuysen, 1873.   316 p.   (1820-
     1873)

867 Root, E. W. "Some Unprinted Minutes of the Albany
     Common Council. " New York State Historical Asso-
     ciation Journal, 1 (January, 1919), 43-47. (1823)

868 Leonard, James M. "Correspondence and Confrontation
     Between William Duffy, Manager, and John Hamilton,
     Actor. " Theatre Survey, 13 (May, 1972), 42-51.
     (1830's)

869 Smither, Nelle. " 'The Bright Particular Star': Char-
     lotte Cushman in Albany. " New York Public Library
     Bulletin, 71 (November, 1967), 563-572. (1836-1837)

870 Munsell, Joel. "Tyrone Power's Impressions of Al-
     bany. " Annals of Albany. Albany: J. Munsell,
     1850-1859. Vol. 10, pp. 391-397.

871 _____ . "The Albany Theatre. " Collections on the
     History of Albany. Albany: J. Munsell, 1867. Vol.
     2, pp. 32-67.

872 Brown, William Langdon. "A History of the Leland
     Opera House, Albany, New York, Under the Manage-
     ment of John W. Albaugh, 1873-1881. " M.A. State
     University of New York, Albany, 1972. 234 p.

873 Morehouse, Ward. "Famous American Theatres. " The-
     atre Arts, 41 (October, 1957), 68. (1889-)

     See also 1408.

BALDWINSVILLE

874 Downer, Alan S. "The Howard Opera House (1861-
     1914). " Baldwinsville Gazette, January 2, 1941.

BROOKLYN

875 Leiter, Samuel Louis. "The Legitimate Theatre in
     Brooklyn, 1861-1898. " Ph.D. New York University,
     1968. 2 vols. 635 p. [68-11796]

876 _____ . "Brooklyn as an American Theatre City,
     1861-1898. " Journal of Long Island History, 8 (Win-
     ter-Spring, 1968), 1-11.

877 Harrison, Gabriel. A History of the Progress of the
     Drama, Music and the Fine Arts in the City of
     Brooklyn. Brooklyn, 1884. 64 p.

BUFFALO

878 Smith, Ardis, and Kathryn Smith. Theatre in Early
     Buffalo. Buffalo: Buffalo and Erie County Historical
     Society, 1975. Adventures in Western New York His-
     tory, Vol. 22, 16 p.

879 Strong, Eve E. "The Theatre in Buffalo, New York. "
M. A. University of Michigan, 1943. (1820-1942)

880 Hill, Richmond C. A Thespian Temple: A Brief History of the Academy of Music and Review of Dramatic Events of Over Fifty Years in the City of
Buffalo, New York. Buffalo: Courier Company,
1893. 24 p.

881 Illingwirth, Charles S. "This I Remember--II: The
Theatre in the '90's. " Niagara Frontier, 1 (Spring,
1954), 39-40.

882 _____. "Buffalo Theatres, 1898 to 1908. " Niagara
Frontier, 6 (Summer, 1959), 42-49.

883 Smith, H. Perry. History of the City of Buffalo and
Erie County. Syracuse, N. Y. , 1884. Vol. 2, pp.
542-545.

EAST HAMPTON

884 Huguenin, Charles A. "Jabez Peck, teacher-play-
wright. " Long Island Forum, 19 (November, 1956),
203-204, 212-214. (1786)

ELMIRA

885 Barber, W. Charles. "A Great Show Town: Golden
Age of Elmira's Theaters, Movies. " Chemung Historical Journal, 7 (June, 1962), 975-982.

ITHACA

886 Niedeck, Arthur Ellsworth. "A Sketch of the Theatres
of Ithaca, 1842-1942. " M. A. Cornell University,
1942. 2 vols.

OSWEGO

887 Rickert, Alfred E. "A History of Theatre in Oswego,
New York, from Its Beginning to 1875. " Ph. D.
University of Denver, 1967. 339 p. [67-16605]
(1828-)

OWEGO

888 Kingman, LeRoy Wilson. "Account of Theatrical Ac-

tivities in Owego during the Nineteenth Century. "
Owego: Some Account of the Early Settlement of the
Village in Tioga County, New York.   Owego, New
York: Owego Gazette Office, 1907.   pp. 501-544.

ROCHESTER

889   McKelvey, Blake Faus.   "The Theatre in Rochester
        during Its First Nine Decades. " Rochester History,
        16 (July, 1954), 1-28.   (1824-1915)

890   Bitz, Nellie Edith.   "A Half Century of Theatre in Early
        Rochester. " M. A. Syracuse University, 1941.   161 p.
        (1824-1869)

891   Elwood, George M.   Some Earlier Public Amusements
        of Rochester.   Rochester: Democrat and Chronicle
        Print, 1894.   62 p.

892   King, Rolf.   "Edwin Booth's First Appearances in Roch-
        ester. " Rochester Historical Society, Publication
        Fund Series, 18 (1940), 215-218.   (1850's)

893   Foreman, Edward R.   "Edwin Booth in Rochester. "
        Rochester Historical Society Publication, 5 (1926),
        113-119.

894   King, Rolf.   "Sketches of Early German Influence on
        Rochester's Theatrical and Musical Life. " Ameri-
        can-German Review, 8 (December, 1941), 13-15,
        34.   (1850's)

895   Peck, William Farley.   History of Rochester and Mon-
        roe County New York.   New York and Chicago:
        Pioneer Publishing Co. , 1908.   pp. 181-189.

896   McKelvey, Blake.   Rochester: The Quest for Quality
        1890-1925.   Cambridge, Massachusetts, 1956.   pp.
        214-224.

SYRACUSE

897   Sinnett, Alice Rosemary.   "A Selective Survey of the
        Syracuse Theatre, 1823-1915. " M. A. Syracuse Uni-
        versity, 1952.

898   Chase, Franklin H.   Syracuse and Its Environs.   Sy-
        racuse, N. Y. , 1924.   Vol. 1, pp. 229-245, 247-266.

TROY

899   Ames, Edgar W.   "First Presentation of Uncle Tom's
      Cabin, at the Troy Museum, Troy, New York, Sept.
      27, 1852. " Americana, 6 (November, 1911), 1045-
      1052.

NORTH CAROLINA

ASHEVILLE

900   Dalton, Donald B.   "The History of Theatre in Ashe-
      ville, North Carolina, 1832-1972. " M. A. University
      of North Carolina, Chapel Hill, 1972.

901   Rulfs, Donald J.   "The Theater in Asheville from 1879
      to 1931. " North Carolina Historical Review, 36
      (October, 1959), 429-441.

CHAPEL HILL

902   Henderson, Archibald.   "The First Carolina Players. "
      Carolina Play-Book, 4 (March, 1931), 5-12.   (1786,
      1796-1797)

CHARLOTTE

903   Barber, Rupert T. , Jr.   "A History of the Theatre in
      Charlotte, North Carolina, From 1873-1902. " Ph. D.
      Louisiana State University, 1970.   viii, 356 p.   [71-
      06540]

      See also 920.

FAYETTEVILLE

904   Rulfs, Donald J.   "The Ante-Bellum Professional The-
      ater in Fayetteville. " North Carolina Historical Re-
      view, 31 (April, 1954), 125-133.   (1823-1860)

GREENSBORO

      See 920.

RALEIGH

905　Rulfs, Donald J.　"The Ante-Bellum Professional The-
　　　　ater in Raleigh. "　North Carolina Historical Review,
　　　　29 (July, 1952), 344-358.　(1803-1860)

906　Lemmon, Sarah McCulloh.　"Entertainment in Raleigh
　　　　in 1890. "　North Carolina Historical Review,　40
　　　　(July, 1963), 321-337.

SALISBURY

907　Epperson, James Register.　"The Combination Touring
　　　　Company and Its Influence on the Theatre in Salisbury,
　　　　Rowan County, North Carolina, from 1873-1910. "
　　　　Ph. D. Florida State University, 1977.　v, 397 p.
　　　　[77-24757]

　　See also 920.

WILMINGTON

908　Rulfs, Donald J.　"The Professional Theatre in Wil-
　　　　mington, 1858-1870. "　North Carolina Historical Re-
　　　　view, 28 (April, 1951), 119-136.

909　　　　　　　.　"Famous American Theatres. "　Theatre
　　　　Arts, 42 (June, 1958), 56-57.　(1858-)

910　Wetmore, Thomas H. , Jr.　"The Literary and Cultural
　　　　Development of Ante-Bellum Wilmington, North Car-
　　　　olina. "　M. A. Duke University, 1940.

911　Allen, Nancie W.　"A Record of North Carolina's Thalian
　　　　Hall from 1861 to 1865 as Reflected in The Wilmington
　　　　Daily Journal. "　M. A. University of North Carolina,
　　　　Chapel Hill, 1972.　83 p.

912　Henderson, Archibald.　"The Thalian Association. "
　　　　Carolina Play-Book, 3 (March, 1930), 5-6.

913　Burr, James Guy.　The Thalian Association of Wilming-
　　　　ton, N. C.; With Sketches of Its Members.　Wilming-
　　　　ton:　J. A. Engelhard, 1871.　52 p.

914　Rulfs, Donald J.　"The Professional Theatre in Wilming-
　　　　ton, 1870-1900. "　North Carolina Historical Review,
　　　　28 (July, 1951), 316-331.

See also 1432.

WINSTON-SALEM

915 Reines, Philip. "A Cultural History of the City of Winston-Salem, North Carolina: 1766-1966. " Ph. D.
University of Denver, 1970. 647 p. [71-10240]
(1880 drama-)

See also 920.

GENERAL

916 Henderson, Archibald. "Early Drama and Professional
Entertainment in North Carolina. " Reviewer, 5
(July, 1925), 47-57. (1702-1823)

917 _____. "Strolling Players in Eighteenth Century
North Carolina. " Carolina Play-Book, 15 (March,
1942), 24-26; (June, 1942), 43-46. (1702-1797)

918 Walser, Richard G. "Strolling Players in North Carolina, 1768-1788. " Carolina Play-Book, 10 (December, 1937), 108-109.

919 Henderson, Archibald. "Early Drama and Amateur Entertainment in North Carolina. Part I. " Reviewer,
5 (October, 1925), 68-77. (1787-1847)

920 Rulfs, Donald J. "The Era of the Opera House in
Piedmont, North Carolina. " North Carolina Historical
Review, 35 (July, 1958), 328-346. (Charlotte, Greens-
boro, Salisbury, Winston-Salem) (1873-1930)

See also 1426.

NORTH DAKOTA

BISMARCK

921 Miller, Dale. "A Record of the Theatrical Activity in
Bismarck, Dakota Territory from January 1873 to
June 1886. " M. A. North Dakota State University, 1960.

See also 1447.

FARGO

922   Browning, Richard J.   "A Record of the Professional
         Theatre Activity in Fargo, Dakota Territory from
         1880 through 1888. " M. S. North Dakota State Uni-
         versity, 1958.

923   Bigelow, Edwin L.   "A Record of the Professional The-
         atre Activity in Fargo, North Dakota from 1889
         through 1903. " M. S. North Dakota State University,
         1955.

         See also 1447.

GRAND FORKS

924   Davies, W. P.   "The Early Theatre in Grand Forks. "
         North Dakota Quarterly Journal, 16 (March, 1926),
         242-257.   (1885-)

925   Adair, Alan H.   "History of the Metropolitan Theatre
         in Grand Forks, North Dakota, Under Independent
         Management, 1890-1897. " M. A. University of North
         Dakota, 1970.

926   Tomasek, Paul.   "The Metropolitan Opera House of
         Grand Forks, N. D. " B. A. University of North Da-
         kota, 1971.

         See also 1447.

OHIO

AKRON

927   Nichols, Kenneth L.   "In Order of Appearance: Akron's
         Theaters, 1840-1940. " M. A. University of Akron,
         1968.   138 p.

928   Collins, John D.   "Henry Eugene Abbey, Akron Impre-
         sario. " M. A. University of Akron, 1960.

929 Schwan, Laurine W.   "Amusements and Meeting Places. "
     A Centennial History of Akron, 1825-1925.   Akron,
     Ohio, 1925.   pp. 368-387.

ATHENS

930 Brady, William Henry.   "A History of Theatre at Ohio
     University (1804 to 1920). "   M. F. A.   Ohio University,
     1955.   56 p.

931 Frebault, Hubert J.   "Professional Theatre in Athens,
     Ohio, since 1897. "   M. A.   Ohio University, 1953.
     (-1929)

CINCINNATI

932 Langworthy, Helen.   "The Theatre in the Lower Valley
     of the Ohio, 1797-1860. "   M. A.   University of Iowa,
     1926.   (Frankfort, Lexington, Louisville, Kentucky;
     Nashville, Tennessee; St. Louis, Missouri)

933 Smith, Ophia Delilah.   "The Early Theater of Cincin-
     nati. "   Historical and Philosophical Society of Ohio
     Bulletin, 13 (October, 1955), 231-253.   (1801-1817)

934 _____ .   "The Cincinnati Theater (1817-1830). "   His-
     torical and Philosophical Society of Ohio Bulletin, 14
     (October, 1956), 251-282.

935 Dunlap, James Francis.   "Queen City Stages: Profes-
     sional Dramatic Activity in Cincinnati, 1837-1861. "
     Ph. D.   Ohio State University, 1954.   289 numbered
     pages; 2118 counting unnumbered pages.   [59-02558]

936 Hall, Virginius C.   "A Lithograph Quiz. "   Historical
     and Philosophical Society of Ohio Bulletin, 7 (April,
     1949), 111-115.   (1837-1845)

937 Kellogg, Elizabeth R.   "Amateur Dramatics in Old Cin-
     cinnati. "   Historical and Philosophical Society of
     Ohio Bulletin, 7 (January, 1949), 35-43.   (1840's-)

938 Dunlap, James F.   "Queen City Stages: Highlights of
     the Theatrical Season of 1843. "   Historical and Phil-
     osophical Society of Ohio Bulletin, 19 (April, 1961),
     128-143.

939 Wood, Ralph Charles. "Geschichte des deutschen the-
     aters in Cincinnati. " M. A. University of Cincinnati,
     1930.

940 _____. "Geschichte des Deutschen Theaters von Cin-
     cinnati. " Deutsch-Amerikanische Geschichtblatter,
     32 (1932), 411-522. (1843-)

941 Mead, David. "William Charles Macready and the Cin-
     cinnati Stage. " Historical and Philosophical Society
     of Ohio Bulletin, 11 (April, 1953), 90-98. (1844,
     1849)

942 Starr, Stephen Z. "William Charles Macready vs. Ed-
     win Forrest. " Historical and Philosophical Society
     of Ohio Bulletin, 17 (July, 1959), 167-180. (1844-)

943 Dunlap, James Francis. "Sophisticates and Dupes.
     Cincinnati Audiences, 1851. " Historical and Phil-
     osophical Society of Ohio Bulletin, 13 (April, 1955),
     87-97.

944 Holliday, Joseph E. "Notes on Samuel N. Pike and His
     Opera Houses. " Cincinnati Historical Society Bulle-
     tin, 25 (July, 1967), 165-183. (1857-1869)

945 Swift, Mary Grace. "Terpsichore in the Western Ath-
     ens: Ante-Bellum Ballet in the Queen City. " Cin-
     cinnati Historical Society Bulletin, 35 (Summer, 1977),
     79-.

946 Thompson, Florence L. "The Theatre in Cincinnati,
     Ohio, 1860-1883. " M. A. University of Iowa, 1928.

947 Grandstaff, Russell James. "A History of the Profes-
     sional Theatre in Cincinnati, Ohio, 1861-1886. "
     Ph. D. University of Michigan, Ann Arbor, 1963.   2
     vols. v, 459 p. [64-00817]

948 Wood, Ralph Charles. "Geschichte des deutschen The-
     aters von Cincinnati. History of the German Theater in
     Cincinnati. " Ph. D. Cornell University, 1932.   iii,
     158 p. (1872-1918)

949 Kellogg, Elizabeth R. "Old Theater Programs. " His-
     torical and Philosophical Society of Ohio Bulletin, 6
     (July, 1948), 66-68. (1880-1900)

950   Holliday, Joseph E.   "Cincinnati Opera Festivals During
       the Gilded Age. "   Cincinnati Historical Society Bulle-
       tin, 24 (April, 1966), 131-149.

951   _____.   "Grand Opera Comes to the Zoo. "   Cincinnati
       Historical Society Bulletin, 30 (Spring, 1972), 7-.

952   Spraul, Judith.   "Cultural Boosterism, the Construction
       of Music Hall. "   Cincinnati Historical Society Bulle-
       tin, 34 (Fall, 1976), 189-.

953   Stern, Joseph S. , Jr.   "The Queen of the Queen City:
       Music Hall. "   Cincinnati Historical Society Bulletin,
       31 (Spring, 1977), 7-.

954   Wills, J. Robert.   "Late Nineteenth Century Theatre in
       the Lebanon Opera House. "   Cincinnati Historical So-
       ciety Bulletin, 33 (Summer, 1975), 121-.

955   Dann, Peg.   "The Strobridge Collection. "   Cincinnati
       Historical Society Bulletin, 31 (Winter, 1973), 253-.

956   Goss, Charles Frederic, ed.   Cincinnati, the Queen
       City, 1788-1912.   Chicago: S. J. Clarke Publishing
       Co. , 1912.   Vol. 1, pp. 446-456.

       See also 981.

CLEVELAND

957   Cole, Marion.   "Theatrical and Musical Entertainment
       in Early Cleveland, 1796-1854. "   M. A. Case West-
       ern Reserve University, 1958.   170 p.

958   Gaiser, Gerhard Walter.   "The History of the Cleveland
       Theatre from the Beginning to 1854. "   Ph. D. Uni-
       versity of Iowa, 1953.   2 vols.   699 p.   [00-06509]
       (1815-)

959   Dix, William Shepherd.   "The Theatre in Cleveland,
       Ohio, 1854-1875. "   Ph. D. University of Chicago,
       1946.   496 p.

960   Ezekiel, Margaret Ulmer.   "The History of the Theatre
       in Cleveland: 1875-1885. "   Ph. D. Case Western Re-
       serve University, 1968.   ix, 291 p.   [68-10210]

961 Wiedenthal, Maurice. "The Drama. " A History of
     Cleveland, Ohio by Samuel Peter Orth. Chicago &
     Cleveland: S. J. Clarke Publishing Co. , 1910. Vol.
     1, pp. 434-449.

See also 981.

COLUMBUS

962 Clifton, Lucile. "The Early Theater in Columbus,
     Ohio, 1820-1840. " Ohio State Archaeological and
     Historical Quarterly, 62 (July, 1953), 234-246.

963 Utz, Kathryn Elizabeth. "Columbus, Ohio, Theatre
     Seasons 1840-41 to 1860-61. " Ph. D. Ohio State Uni-
     versity, 1952. 2 vols. viii, 890 p. [59-06611]

964 Burbick, William George. "Columbus, Ohio Theatre
     From the Beginning of the Civil War to 1875. " Ph. D.
     Ohio State University, 1963. ii, 369 p. [64-06999]
     (1861-)

965 Siena, Marcia Ann. "The History of the Great South-
     ern Theater, Columbus, Ohio. " M. A. Ohio State
     University, 1957. (1894-1913)

966 Prugh, Dan F. "A History of the Famous Columbus
     Metropolitan Opera House. " Franklin County His-
     torical Society Bulletin, 3 (1950-1951), 18-19.

967 Moore, Opha. History of Franklin County, Ohio. To-
     peka, Kansas & Indianapolis: Historical Publishing
     Co. , 1930. Vol. 1, pp. 386-398.

See also 981.

DELAWARE

968 Griffith, Max Eugene. "The Delaware, Ohio, City Op-
     era House and Its Nineteenth Century Activities. "
     M. A. Ohio State University, 1968. (1882-1899)

FREMONT

969 Miesle, Frank L. "A History of the Opera House at
     Fremont, Ohio, from 1890 to 1900. " M. A. Bowling
     Green State University, 1948.

NELSONVILLE

970 Steenrod, Spencer. "A History of Stuart's Opera House,
        Nelsonville, Ohio." M.A. Ohio University, 1973.
        (1879-1924)

NEW CONCORD

971 Swiss, Cheryl D. "A History of Theatre at Muskingum
        College." M.A. Ohio University, 1972. (1837-1972)

PENINSULA

     See 1471.

SALEM

972 Cassady, Marshall G. "The History of Professional
        Theatre in Salem, Ohio, 1847-1894." Ph.D. Kent
        State University, 1972. 361 p. [72-22425]

SPRINGFIELD

973 Prince, Benjamin F., ed. A Standard History of Spring-
        field and Clark County, Ohio. Chicago and New
        York: The American Historical Society, 1922. Vol.
        1, pp. 432-436.

TOLEDO

974 Stolzenbach, Norma Frizzelle. "The History of the The-
        atre in Toledo, Ohio, from Its Beginnings until
        1893." Ph.D. University of Michigan, Ann Arbor,
        1954. vii, 331 p. [00-08418] (1833-)

975 Revett, Marion S. "The Old Stage Door." Northwest
        Ohio Quarterly, 23 (Summer, 1951), 152-157. (1850-
        1895)

976 Stolzenbach, Norma Frizzelle. "The Wheeler Opera
        House." Northwest Ohio Quarterly, 26 (Summer,
        1954), 210-257. (1871-1893)

977 Orians, G. Harrison. "History of the Burt Theatre
        in Toledo." Northwest Ohio Quarterly, 33 (Spring,
        1961), 60-80. (1898-1904)

YOUNGSTOWN

978 Wilson, Bertha Amelia. "A History of the Theatre in
     Youngstown, Ohio. " M. A. University of Michigan,
     Ann Arbor, 1945. (19th century)

ZANESVILLE

979 Merrick, Mary Louise. "A History of the Theatre of
     Zanesville, Ohio, between the Years of 1831 and
     1866. " M. A. Ohio State University, 1941.

GENERAL

980 Eyssen, Donald Chester. "The Theatre in Ohio, 1800-
     1890. " M. A. Ohio Wesleyan University, 1934.

981 Harris, Geraldine Caroline. "A History of the Theatre
     in Ohio, 1815-1880. " M. A. Ohio State University,
     1937. (Cincinnati, Cleveland, Columbus)

982 Miller, William Marion, and Phillis J. Heckathorn.
     "Sarah Bernhardt in Ohio. " French Review, 26
     (October, 1952), 32-39. (1881-)

OKLAHOMA

OKLAHOMA CITY

983 Gober, Ruth Bell. "The Professional Theatre in Okla-
     homa City, 1889-1941. " M. A. Northwestern Uni-
     versity, 1941.

984 Brandes, K. Kay. "Theatrical Activities in Oklahoma
     City from 1889 to 1964. " M. F. A. University of
     Oklahoma, Norman, 1964.

985 Shirk, Lucyl. "Early Day Theater. " Oklahoma City:
     Capitol of Soonerland. Oklahoma City, Oklahoma:
     Oklahoma City Board of Education, 1957. pp. 157-
     159.

GENERAL

986 Nolan, Paul T. "The Boomers: Oklahoma Playwrights
Opened the Territory." Chronicles of Oklahoma, 41
(Autumn, 1963), 248-252. (1896-1919)

OREGON

BAKER

See 999.

EUGENE

987 Ernst, Alice Henson. "Eugene's Theatres and 'Shows'
in Horse and Buggy Days, Part I: 1852-1884."
Oregon Historical Quarterly, 44 (June, 1943), 127-
139.

988 White, Irle E. "The Development of Educational Theatre at the University Level as Exemplified by the
Dramatic Activity at the University of Oregon, 1872-
1962." M.S. University of Oregon, 1962.

989 Ernst, Alice Henson. "Eugene's Theatres and 'Shows'
in Horse and Buggy Days, Part II: 1884-1903."
Oregon Historical Quarterly, 44 (September, 1943),
232-248.

FORT VANCOUVER

See 996.

LA GRANDE

See 999.

PORTLAND

990 Schilling, Lester Lorenzo. "The History of the Theatre in Portland, Oregon, 1846-1959." Ph.D. University of Wisconsin, Madison, 1961. iv, 501 p.
[61-01553]

991 Larson, Patricia Mary. "A Study of the Museum The-
      atre in the United States Including an Analysis of the
      Museum Theatre in Portland, Oregon." M. A. Uni-
      versity of Oregon, 1964. 134 p. [M-609] (1880's)

     See also 996.

SALEM

992 Maxwell, Ben. "A Hundred Years of Salem Theatrical
      History." Marion County History, 4 (1958), 25-29.
      (1856-1958)

993 Patton, E. Cooke. "Early Theatrical History of Sa-
      lem." Oregon Magazine, 6 (1922), 20-21.

994 Maxwell, Ben. "Salem Theaters Center of Interesting
      History." Capital Journal, February 5, 1953, p.
      17.

THE DALLES

     See 996, 999.

GENERAL

995 Ernst, Alice Henson. "First Curtains in a Last Fron-
      tier." Northwest Review, 3 (Fall-Winter, 1959),
      29-32. (1846)

996 _____. "Stage Annals of Early Oregon from 1846
      to 1875." Oregon Historical Quarterly, 42 (June,
      1941), 151-161. (Fort Vancouver, Portland, The
      Dalles)

997 _____. Trouping in the Oregon Country. Portland:
      Oregon Historical Society, 1961. 197 p. (1846-)

998 Clark, Dan E. "Pioneer Pastimes." Oregon Historical
      Quarterly, 57 (December, 1956), 333-349. (1850's)

999 Hiatt, Richard Gordon. "A History of Theatrical Ac-
      tivity on the Oregon Trail (Boise, Idaho, to The
      Dalles, Oregon: 1880-1910)." Ph. D. Brigham
      Young University, 1974. 363 p. [74-17934] (Ba-
      ker, La Grande, The Dalles)

1000   Ernst, Alice Henson.   "Homer Davenport on Stage. "
       Oregon Historical Quarterly, 66 (March, 1965), 39-
       50.   (1890's)

1001   Oregon: End of the Trail.   Portland: Binfords, 1940.
       pp. 119-123; rev. ed. , 1951.

1002   Peterson, Emil R. , and Alfred Powers.   A Century
       of Coos and Curry: History of Southwest Oregon.
       Portland: Binfords & Mort, 1952.   Chapter 22.

1003   Ernst, Alice Henson.   "Early Day Theaters. "   Port-
       land Sunday Oregonian, October 12, 1947, pp. 1,
       6.

1004   Marks, Arnold.   "Our Historic Theatres. "   Portland
       Journal, November 6, 1955, mag. sec. , pp. 14,
       15.

       See also 1451, 1454.

PENNSYLVANIA

HARRISBURG

1005   Struble, George I.   "A Fellow of Infinite Jest: The
       Sad Last Days of a Great Comedian in Harrisburg. "
       Commonwealth, 2 (February, 1948), 16-18.   (Jo-
       seph Jefferson)   (1832)

JOHNSTOWN

1006   Koontz, John G.   "A History of the Theater in Johns-
       town, Pennsylvania, 1890-1900. "   M. A. University
       of Pittsburgh, 1952.

LANCASTER

1007   Reichmann, Felix.   "Amusements in Lancaster, 1750-
       1940. "   Lancaster County Historical Society Papers,
       45 (1941), 25-56.

1008 Worner, William Frederic. "The Earliest Known Ad-
      vertisement of a Theatrical Performance in Lan-
      caster. " Lancaster County Historical Society Pa-
      pers, 28 (1924), 30-35. (1791)

1009 Diffenderffer, Frank R. , and Samuel M. Sener. "Early
      Lancaster Playbills and Playhouses. " Lancaster
      County Historical Society Papers, 7 (1903), 24-45.
      (1800-)

1010 Worner, William Frederic. "The Thespian Society. "
      Lancaster County Historical Society Papers, 34
      (1930), 38-43. (1818-1829)

1011 _____. "Theatre on West Chestnut Street, Lan-
      caster. " Lancaster County Historical Society Pa-
      pers, 37 (1933), 161-172. (1830-)

1012 _____. "Charlotte Cushman in Lancaster. " Lan-
      caster County Historical Society Papers, 34 (1930),
      169-175. (1841)

1013 Diffenderffer, Frank R. "Early Lancaster Theatre. "
      Lancaster County Historical Society Papers, 10
      (1906), 114-119. (1843)

1014 Worner, William Frederic. "Fanny Kemble in Lan-
      caster. " Lancaster County Historical Society Pa-
      pers, 36 (1932), 157-158. (1849)

1015 Greiner, Tyler L. "A History of Professional Enter-
      tainment at the Fulton Opera House in Lancaster,
      Pennsylvania, 1852-1930. " M. A. Pennsylvania
      State University, 1977. 2 vols. 859 p.

1016 Kingston, Joseph T. "History of Fulton Opera House. "
      Lancaster County Historical Society Papers, 56
      (1952), 141-154. (1852-1952)

1017 Hager, Walter C. "Fulton Hall and Its Graven Im-
      age. " Lancaster County Historical Society Papers,
      22 (1918), 141-148. (1852-)

1018 Burns, Doris. "Reminiscences of the Fulton Opera
      House. " Journal of the Lancaster County Historical
      Society, 76 (Trinity, 1972), 117-135. (1853-1930)

MAHONEY CITY

1019   Beegle, Joanne Pangonis.   "A History of Kaier's
        Grand Opera House. "   M. A. Pennsylvania State
        University, 1964.   (1885-1913)

MEADVILLE

1020   Engel, Bernard B.   "Chronicles of the Meadville Stage:
        1800-1899. "   Ph. D. University of Pittsburgh, 1968.
        2 vols. 845 p.   [68-13973]

PHILADELPHIA

1021   Stine, Richard Denzler.   "The Philadelphia Theater,
        1682-1829: Its Growth as a Cultural Institution. "
        Ph. D. University of Pennsylvania, 1951. 215 p.

1022   Dye, William S. , Jr.   "Pennsylvania versus the The-
        atre. "   Pennsylvania Magazine of History and Bi-
        ograpy, 55 (October, 1931), 333-372.   (1682-1794)

1023   Quigley, Bernard J.   "First Seasons in Philadelphia:
        A Study of the Philadelphia Stage, 1682-1767. "
        M. A. Catholic University of America, 1951.

1024   Shiffler, Harrold C.   "Religious Opposition to the
        Eighteenth Century Philadelphia Stage. "   Educational
        Theatre Journal, 14 (October, 1962), 215-223.
        (1686-1793)

1025   Pollock, Thomas Clark.   "The Philadelphia Stage Dur-
        ing the Eighteenth Century. "   Ph. D. University of
        Pennsylvania, 1930. 67 p.   (1723-1799)

1026   _____. The Philadelphia Theatre in the Eighteenth
        Century, Together with the Day Book of the Same
        Period. Philadelphia: University of Pennsylvania
        Press, 1933. 445 p.   (1723-1799)

1027   Lees, C. Lowell.   "First Nighters of Eighteenth Cen-
        tury America: II. The East ... Philadelphia. "
        Players Magazine, 12 (January-February, 1936),
        5-6, 28-30.   (1742-)

1028   Durang, Charles.   "The Philadelphia Stage, From the
        Year 1749 to the Year 1855, etc. "   Philadelphia
        Sunday Dispatch, First Series (1749-1821), May 7,

1854, and following issues; Second Series, (1822-1830), June 29, 1856 and following issues; Third Series (1831-1855), July 8, 1860, and following issues.

1029 Quinn, Arthur Hobson. "The Theatre and the Drama in Old Philadelphia." Transactions of the American Philosophical Society, 43 (March, 1953), 313-317. (1749-1830)

1030 Gegenheimer, Albert Frank. "Thomas Godfrey: Protégé of William Smith." Pennsylvania History, 9 (October, 1942), 233-251. (1749-)

1031 Jackson, Joseph. "The Shakespeare Tradition in Philadelphia." Pennsylvania Magazine of History and Biography, 40 (April, 1916), 161-171. (1749-1851)

1032 Quinn, Arthur Hobson. "The Authorship of the First American College Masque." General Magazine, 28 (April, 1926), 313-316. (1757)

1033 Holmes, Charles Nevers. "America's First Permanent Playhouse." The Drama, 9 (February, 1919), 103-109. (1766-1821)

1034 "America's First Theatre." The Theatre, 16 (July, 1912), 16. (1766-)

1035 Yalof, Helen Roberta. "British Military Theatricals in Philadelphia During the Revolutionary War." Ph.D. New York University, 1972. 226 p. [72-26624] (1777-1778)

1036 Brown, Jared A. "'Howe's Strolling Company': British Military Theatre in New York and Philadelphia, 1777 and 1778." Theatre Survey, 18 (May, 1977), 30-43.

1037 Pattee, Fred Lewis. "The British Theatre in Philadelphia in 1778." American Literature, 6 (January, 1935), 381-388.

1038 Pollock, Thomas Clark. "Notes on Professor Pattee's 'The British Theatre in Philadelphia in 1778.'" American Literature, 7 (November, 1935), 310-314.

1039   Geib, George W.   "Playhouses and Politics: Lewis
       Hallam and the Confederation Theater. "   Journal
       of Popular Culture, 5 (Fall, 1971), 324-339. (1779-
       1789)

1040   Anderson, Gillian B.   " 'The Temple of Minerva' and
       Francis Hopkinson: A Reappraisal of America's
       First Poet-Composer. "   Proceedings of the Amer-
       ican Philosophical Society, 120 (June, 1976), 166-
       177. (1781)

1041   Spell, Jefferson R.   "Hispanic Contributions to the
       Early Theatre in Philadelphia. "   Hispanic Review,
       9 (January, 1941), 192-198. (1783-1808)

1042   Paul, Henry N.   "Shakespeare in Philadelphia. "   Amer-
       ican Philosophical Society Proceedings, 76 (1936),
       719-729. (1788-)

1043   Haney, John L.   "Shakespeare and Philadelphia. "
       Philadelphia City Historical Society Publication, 4
       (1936), 37-74.

1044   Schoenberger, Harold William.   "American Adaptations
       of French Plays on the New York and Philadelphia
       Stages from 1790 to 1833. "   Ph. D. University of
       Pennsylvania, 1924.

1045   _____.   American Adaptations of French Plays on
       the New York and Philadelphia Stages from 1790
       to 1833.   Philadelphia, 1924.

1046   McKenzie, Ruth Harsha.   "Organization, Production,
       and Management at the Chestnut Street Theatre,
       Philadelphia, from 1791 to 1820. "   Ph. D. Stanford
       University, 1952.   ix, 332 p.

1047   Wolcott, John Rutherford.   "Philadelphia's Chestnut
       Street Theatre: A Plan and Elevation. "   Journal
       of the Society of Architectural Historians, 30 (Oc-
       tober, 1971), 209-218.   (1792-1805)

1048   _____.   "English Influences on American Staging
       Practice: A Case Study of the Chestnut Street
       Theatre, Philadelphia, 1794-1820. "   Ph. D. Ohio
       State University, 1967.   2 vols.   xviii, 486 p.
       [68-03091]

1049 Herr, John Harold. "Thomas Wignell and the Chesnut
      Street Theatre." Ph.D. Michigan State University,
      1969. 323 p. [70-09558] (1794-1803)

1050 Brede, Charles Frederic. "The German Drama in
      English on the Philadelphia Stage From 1794 to
      1830. Preceded by a General Account of the The-
      atre in Philadelphia From 1794-96." Ph.D. Uni-
      versity of Pennsylvania, 1905. 293 p.

1051   . The German Drama in English on the Phila-
      delphia Stage from 1794 to 1830, Preceded by a
      General Account of the Theatre in Philadelphia from
      1749-1796. Philadelphia: Americana Germanica
      Press, 1918. 295 p.

1052   . "The German Drama in English on the Phila-
      delphia Stage." German American Annals, New
      Series, 10 (1912), 3-64, 99-149, 226-248; 11 (1913),
      64-99, 175-202; 13 (1915), 69-97; 14 (1916), 69-
      110.

1053   . "Schiller on the Philadelphia Stage to the
      Year 1830." German American Annals, 3 (1950),
      254-275.

1054 Needle, Harold Fischer. "The Plays of August von
      Kotzebue on the New York and Philadelphia Stages."
      M.A. Pennsylvania State University, 1934.

1055 Huch, C.F. "Das Deutsche Theater in Philadelphia
      vor dem Bürgerkriege." Deutscher Pionier-Verein
      von Philadelphia Mitteilungen, 6 (1907), 13-25.

1056   . "Das Deutsche Theater in Philadelphia
      während des Bürgerkrieges." Deutscher Pionier-
      Verein von Philadelphia Mitteilungen, 7 (1908), 10-
      20.

1057   . "Das Deutsche Theater in Philadelphia seit
      dem Bürgerkriege." Deutscher Pionier-Verein von
      Philadelphia Mitteilungen, 8 (1908), 14-27.

1058 Adams, M. Ray. "Robert Merry and the American
      Theatre." Theatre Survey, 6 (May, 1965), 1-11.
      (1796-1799)

1059 Herr, John H. "The Bankruptcy of the Chestnut Street
      Theatre, Philadelphia, 1799. " Theatre Research,
      11 (1971), 154-172.

1060 James, Reese Davis. "Old Drury of Philadelphia: A
      History of the Philadelphia Theatre, 1800-1835. "
      Ph. D. University of Pennsylvania, 1930. 694 p.

1061 _____ . Old Drury of Philadelphia: A History of
      the Philadelphia Stage, 1800-1835, Including the
      Diary or Daily Account Book of William Burke
      Wood, Co-Manager with William Warren of the
      Chestnut Street Theatre, Familiarly Known as Old
      Drury. Philadelphia: University of Pennsylvania
      Press, 1932. 694 p.

1062 _____ . Cradle of Culture, 1800-1810: The Phila-
      delphia Stage. Philadelphia: University of Pennsyl-
      vania Press, 1957. 156 p.

1063 _____ . "The Carriage Waits Without. Milady At-
      tends the Theatre in Philadelphia a Hundred Years
      Ago. " Philadelphia Forum Magazine, 12 (January,
      1933).

1064 _____ . "Yoricks of Yesterday. Twelve Good Men
      and True Who Trod the Philadelphia Stage Over a
      Century Ago. " Philadelphia Forum Magazine, 19
      (April, 1940).

1065 _____ . "Our Early Theatre of Democracy. Thirty
      Years of Growing Pains in the Philadelphia Play
      Houses. " Philadelphia Forum Magazine, 21 (April,
      1942).

1066 _____ . "The First Chestnut Street Theatre. " Phila-
      delphia Forum Magazine, 24 (June, 1945).

1067 Pritner, Calvin Lee. "William Warren's Management
      of the Chestnut Street Theatre Company. " Ph. D.
      University of Illinois, Urbana, 1964. iv, 186 p.
      [65-03659] (1805-1829)

1068 _____ . "A Theater and Its Audience. " Pennsyl-
      vania Magazine of History and Biography, 91 (Jan-
      uary, 1967), 72-79. (1805-1829)

1069 _____. "William Warren's Financial Arrangements
With Traveling Stars--1805-1829. " Theatre Survey,
6 (November, 1965), 83-90.

1070 Dieck, Herman L. "Centenary of America's Oldest
Playhouse. " The Theatre, 8 (April, 1908), 98-100.

1071 Emery, George M. "Passing of America's Oldest Playhouse. " Theatre, 31 (June, 1920), 506-508, 572.
(1809-)

1072 "Theatrical Journal for March, 1811. " The Mirror of
Taste and Dramatic Censor, 3 (March, 1911), 178-
200.

1073 Jackson, Joseph. "Vauxhall Garden. " Pennsylvania
Magazine of History and Biography, 57 (1933), 289-
298. (1814-1819)

1074 Wolcott, John R. "The Genesis of Gas Lights. " Theatre Research, 12 (1972), 74-87. (1816-)

1075 Curtis, John. "A Century of Grand Opera in Philadelphia. " Pennsylvania Magazine of History and Biography, 44 (1920), 122-158. (1818-)

1076 Sprague, Arthur Colby. "The First American Performance of Richard II. " Shakespeare Association
Bulletin, 19 (July, 1944), 110-116. (1819)

1077 Webb, Dorothy Louise Beck. "The Early History of
the Arch Street Theatre, 1828-1834. " Ph. D. Indiana University, 1970. 390 p. [70-26956]

1078 Ware, Ralph Hartman. "American Adaptations of
French Plays on the New York and Philadelphia
Stages from 1834 to the Civil War. " Ph. D. Uni-
versity of Pennsylvania, 1930.

1079 _____. American Adaptations of French Plays on
the New York and Philadelphia Stages from 1834
to the Civil War. Philadelphia: University of
Pennsylvania Press, 1930. 138 p.

1080 Wilson, Arthur Herman. "A History of Philadelphia
Theatre, 1835-1855. " Ph. D. University of Pennsylvania, 1931. 724 p.

1081 _____ . A History of the Philadelphia Theatre, 1835 to 1855. Philadelphia: University of Pennsylvania Press, 1935. 724 p.

1082 Lewis, Orlando Faulkland. "Performances of German Drama in Philadelphia, 1842-1898, as Advertised in Philadelphia Demokrat. " Ph. D. University of Pennsylvania, 1900. 97 p.

1083 Coder, William Dickey. "A History of the Philadelphia Theater, 1856 to 1878. " Ph. D. University of Pennsylvania, 1936. 244 p.

1084 History and Description of the Opera House, or American Academy of Music in Philadelphia. Philadelphia: G. André and Co. , 1857. 20 p.

1085 Robinson, Wayne. "Famous American Theatres. " Theatre Arts, 41 (January, 1957), 67, 95. (1857)

1086 _____ . "Theatre, Philadelphia. " Theatre Arts, 44 (February, 1960), 73-77.

1087 Marshall, Thomas Frederic. "A History of the Philadelphia Theater, 1878-1890. " Ph. D. University of Pennsylvania, 1941. 309 p.

1088 _____ . A History of the Philadelphia Theatre, 1878-1890. Philadelphia, 1943. 54 p. (1878-1879)

1089 The Theatres and Public Halls of Philadelphia. Philadelphia, 188?

1090 Wiedersheim, William A. , II. "Mask and Wig: Retrospect and Prospects. " The General Magazine and Historical Chronicle, 51 (Summer, 1949), 156-162. (1889-)

1091 Potts, Edgar Leroy. "The History of the Philadelphia Theater, 1890-1900. " Ph. D. University of Pennsylvania, 1932.

1092 Lippincott, Horace Mather. "Amusements in the Nineties. " The General Magazine and Historical Chronicle, 52 (Summer, 1950), 239-251. (1893-1897)

1093 MacLeish, Archibald. "The First American Ballet. "
     Living Age, 348 (March, 1935), 87-88.

1094 Dale, Karin. "Indigenous Drama. " Arts in Philadel-
     phia, 2 (November, 1939), 7-8, 31.

1095 Scharf, J. Thomas, and Thompson Westcott. History
     of Philadelphia 1609-1884. Vol. 3, pp. 964-980.

     See also 1407, 1408, 1411, 1413.

PITHOLE

1096 Clark, Frank M. "The Theatre of Pithole, Pennsylva-
     nia, Oil Boom Town. " Western Pennsylvania His-
     torical Magazine, 56 (January, 1973), 39-57. (1865-
     1867)

PITTSBURGH

1097 Anderson, Edward P. "The Intellectual Life of Pitts-
     burgh, 1786-1836: The Theatre. " Western Pennsyl-
     vania Historical Magazine, 14 (July, 1931), 225-232.

1098 Fletcher, Edward Garland. "Records and History of
     Theatrical Activities in Pittsburgh, Pennsylvania,
     From Their Beginnings to 1861. " Ph. D. Harvard
     University, 1931. 2 vols. 614 p. (1790-)

1099 Calvin, Judith Sylvia. "A History of the Showboat The-
     atre on the Northern Rivers. " M. A. Pennsylvania
     State University, 1960. (1815-1960)

1100 Krich, John F. "The Amiable Lady Charms the Iron
     City: Adah Isaacs Menken in Pittsburgh. " Western
     Pennsylvania Historical Magazine, 51 (July, 1968),
     259-278. (1859-1862)

1101 Lowrie, James Allison. "A History of the Pittsburgh
     Stage (1861-1891). " Ph. D. University of Pittsburgh,
     1943. 2 vols. 819 p.

1102 Peebles, Sheila E. "A History of the Pittsburgh Stage,
     1891-1896. " M. A. Kent State University, 1973.

1103 Boucher, John N. A Century and a Half of Pittsburgh
     and Her People. New York, 1908. Vol. 2, Chap-
     ter 32.

POTTSVILLE

1104   Hobbs, Herrwood E.   "The Theatrical History of Potts-
       ville. "   Publications of the Historical Society of
       Schuylkill County, 6, No. 2 (1950), 5-40.   (1876-
       1950)

READING

1105   Buttorff, Jane.   "A Survey of Theatre in Reading un-
       til 1851. "   Berks County Historical Review, 6
       (1940), 9-15.

1106   Glase, Paul E.   "Annals of the Reading Stage: Early
       Theatre and Playbills. "   Berks County Historical
       Review, 12 (1946-1947), 5-10, 39-47, 75-84, 107-
       115.   (-1917)

1107   _____ .   Annals of the Reading Theatre, 1791-1948.
       Ed. by Milton W. Hamilton.   Reading, Pennsylvania,
       1948.   88 p.

1108   McClellan, Mabel M. K.   "The Glase Theatre Collec-
       tion. "   Historical Review of Berks County, 22 (1956-
       1957), 10-13, 29-31.

TIDIOUTE

1109   Marsh, John L.   "Troupers at Tidioute. "   Players,
       47 (February-March, 1972), 138-144.   (1870-)

TITUSVILLE

1110   Copeland, Bob Herbert.   "The Oil Circuit: A History
       of Professional Theatre in the Oil Region of North-
       western Pennsylvania from 1859 to 1900. "   Ph. D.
       University of Denver, 1969.   390 p.   [70-15447]

WARREN

1111   Marsh, John L.   "Mr. Hall's Hall, an Unlovely Relic
       of Opera-House America. "   Western Pennsylvania
       Historical Magazine, 57 (April, 1974), 167-197.
       (1869-1883)

GENERAL

1112   Little, Paul Judson.   "Reactions to the Theatre: Vir-

ginia, Massachusetts, and Pennsylvania, 1665-1793. "
Ph. D. Syracuse University, 1969. 217 p. [70-
12789]

1113 Maxfield, Ezra Kempton. "Friendly Testimony Re-
garding Stage Plays. " Bulletin of Friends' Historical Association, 14 (Spring, 1925), 13-21; (Autumn, 1925), 53-61. (1720-1925)

1114 Miller, Ernest C. "John Wilkes Booth in the Pennsylvania Oil Region. " The Western Pennsylvania Historical Magazine, 31 (March-June, 1948), 26-47.
(1864)

RHODE ISLAND

NEWPORT

1115 M. , J. E. "The Theatre in Newport, 1761. " Magazine of American History, 3 (October, 1879), 638.

See also 1120, 1121, 1122, 1408.

PROVIDENCE

1116 Blake, Charles. An Historical Account of the Providence Stage: Being a Paper Read Before the Rhode
Island Historical Society, October 25th, 1860.
(With Additions). Providence: George H. Whitney,
1868. 297 p. (1745-1860)

1117 Willard, George Owen. History of the Providence
Stage, 1762-1891. Including Sketches of Many
Prominent Actors Who Have Appeared in America.
Providence: The Rhode Island News Company,
1891. 298 p. (primarily a duplicate of 1116)

1118 Damon, S. Foster. "Providence Theatricals in 1773. "
Rhode Island History, 4 (April, 1945), 55-58.

1119 Halpert, Harold Karl. "Early College Performances
of Otway in Providence. " Rhode Island Historical

Society Collections, 23 (April, 1930), 33-41. (1785,
1792)

See also 1120, 1121, 1122, 1408, 1413.

GENERAL

1120 Brown, Benjamin W. "The Colonial Theatre in New
       England. " Newport Historical Society. Special
       Bulletin, No. 76 (July, 1930), 1-26. (Newport,
       Providence) (1761-1762)

1121 Sherman, Constance D. "The Theatre in Rhode Island
       Before the Revolution. " Rhode Island History, 17
       (January, 1958), 10-14. (Newport, Providence)
       (1761-1762)

1122 Mullin, Donald C. "Early Theatres in Rhode Island. "
       Theatre Survey, 11 (November, 1970), 167-186.
       (Newport, Providence) (1761-1832)

1123 Belcher, Horace G. "Mr. Tambo and Mr. Bones:
       Rhode Island in Negro Minstrelsy. " Rhode Island
       History, 8 (October, 1949), 97-111. (1843-1917)

SOUTH CAROLINA

CHARLESTON

1124 Curtis, Mary Julia. "The Early Charleston Stage:
       1703-1798. " Ph. D. Indiana University, 1968.
       476 p. [68-13699]

1125 Robinson, Emmett. A Guide to the Dock Street The-
       atre and Brief Resume of the Theatres in Charles-
       ton, S. C. from 1730. Charleston: The Footlight
       Players, 1963. 14 p.

1126 Cohen, Hennig. The South Carolina Gazette 1732-
       1775. Columbia, South Carolina: University of
       South Carolina Press, 1953. Chapter 10.

1127 Willis, Eola. The Charleston Stage in the XVIII Century, with Social Settings of the Time. Columbia, South Carolina: The State Company, 1924. 483 p. (1734-1801)

1128 Allen, Hervey. "America's First Theatre: A Rime of Olde Charles-Towne." Theatre Arts, 9 (July, 1925), 467-469. (1734)

1129 Law, Robert Adger. "Early American Prologues and Epilogues." Nation, 98 (April 23, 1914), 463-464. (1734)

1130 _____. "News for Bibliophiles." Nation, 96 (February 27, 1913), 201. (1735-1773)

1131 _____. "Charleston Theatres, 1735-1766." Nation, 99 (September 3, 1914), 278-279.

1132 Lees, C. Lowell. "First Nighters of Eighteenth Century America: I. The South ... Charleston." Players Magazine, 12 (November-December, 1935), 4, 35-37. (1735-)

1133 St. John, James Ivan. "Belles Lettres in Colonial Charleston: A Study of Its Poetry and Drama." M.A. University of South Carolina, Columbia, 1969. (1735-1774)

1134 "Oldest Theatre." Time, 30 (December 6, 1937), 41-42.

1135 "First U.S. Theatre Is Restored." Life, 3 (December 20, 1937), 49-50.

1136 "Charleston Opens Historic Playhouse with Historic Play." Architectural Record, 83 (January, 1938), 20-25. (1736, 1806)

1137 Heyward, DuBose. "Dock Street Theatre." Magazine of Art, 31 (January, 1938), 10-15. (1736)

1138 Roberts, Daisy M. "The Dock Street Theatre Rebuilt--A Federal Project." Scholastic, 31 (January 15, 1938), 10-11.

1139 Vale, Margaret. "Dock Street Theatre..." South Carolina Magazine, 4 (Spring, 1941), 29.

South Carolina   128

1140 Hoole, William Stanley. "Charleston Theatres. " South-
      west Review, 25 (January, 1940), 193-204. (1736-
      1860)

1141 Curtis, Mary Julia. "Charles-Town's Church Street
      Theater. " South Carolina Historical Magazine, 70
      (July, 1969), 149-154. (1763-1774)

1142 Cohen, Hennig. "Shakespeare in Charleston on the Eve
      of the Revolution. " Shakespeare Quarterly, 4 (July,
      1953), 327-330. (1764-1774)

1143 Law, Robert Adger. "A Diversion for Colonial Gentle-
      men. " Texas Review, 2 (July, 1916), 79-88.

1144 Hoole, William Stanley. "Two Famous Theatres of the
      Old South. " South Atlantic Quarterly, 36 (July,
      1937), 273-277. (1792-1861)

1145 Curtis, Julia. "The Architecture and Appearance of
      the Charleston Theatre: 1793-1833. " Educational
      Theatre Journal, 23 (March, 1971), 1-12.

1146 _____. "John Joseph Stephen Leger Sollee and the
      Charleston Theatre. " Educational Theatre Journal,
      21 (October, 1969), 285-298. (1794-1798)

1147 Seeber, Edward D. "The French Theatre in Charleston
      in the Eighteenth Century. " South Carolina His-
      torical and Geneological Magazine, 42 (January,
      1941), 1-7. (1794-)

1148 Watson, Charles S. Antebellum Charleston Dramatists.
      University: University of Alabama Press, 1976.
      183 p. (1797-)

1149 Hoole, William Stanley. "A History of the Charleston
      Theatres, 1800-1875. " M. A. North Texas State
      University, 1941.

1150 _____. The Ante-Bellum Charleston Theatre. Uni-
      versity, Alabama: University of Alabama Press,
      1946. 230 p. (1800-1861)

1151 _____. "Shakspere on the Ante-Bellum Charleston
      Stage. " Shakespeare Association Bulletin, 21 (Jan-
      uary, 1946), 37-45. (1800-1860)

1152 Robinson, Emmett, ed. "Dr. Irving's Reminiscences
      of the Charleston Stage." South Carolina Historical
      and Genealogical Magazine, 51 (July, 1950), 125-131;
      (October, 1950), 195-215; 52 (January, 1951), 26-
      33; (April, 1951), 93-106; (July, 1951), 166-179;
      (October, 1951), 225-232; 53 (January, 1952), 37-
      47. (1800-1859)

1153 Harbin, Billy J. "Hodgkinson's Last Years: At the
      Charleston Theatre, 1803-1805." Theatre Survey,
      13 (November, 1972), 20-43.

1154 Watson, Charles S. "Stephen Cullen Carpenter, First
      Drama Critic of the Charleston Courier." South
      Carolina Historical Magazine, 69 (October, 1968),
      243-252. (1803-1806)

1155 _____. "Jeffersonian Republicanism in William
      Ioor's Independence, the First Play of South Caro-
      lina." South Carolina Historical Magazine, 69
      (July, 1968), 194-203. (1805)

1156 Stephenson, Nan Louise. "The Charleston Theatre
      Management of Joseph George Holman, 1815 to
      1817." M.A. Louisiana State University, 1976.

1157 Ketchum, Barbara. "Actors in the Charleston The-
      atre, 1837-1861." M.A. University of Texas,
      Austin, 1942.

1158 Moehlenbrock, Arthur H. "Kotzebue on the Charles-
      ton Stage." Furman Studies, 34 (1951), 22-31.

1159 _____. "The German Drama on the Charleston
      Stage." Furman Studies, N.S. 1 (Spring, 1954),
      32-39.

1160 Hoole, William Stanley. "Charleston Theatricals Dur-
      ing the Tragic Decade, 1860-1869." Journal of
      Southern History, 11 (November, 1945), 538-547.

      See also 1407, 1408.

GREENVILLE

1161 Richey, Dorothy. "The Arts in Greenville: Theatre
      Arts." Furman Studies, N.S. 7 (November, 1960),
      75-96. (1836-1960)

NEWBERRY

1162   Cox, James Rex.   "The History of the Newberry,
       South Carolina, Opera House, 1880-1973. "   M. A.
       University of South Carolina, Columbia, 1974.
       108 p.

GENERAL

1163   Vale, Margaret.   "Sketches of South Carolina's Role
       in the Theatre. "   South Carolina Magazine, 4 (Win-
       ter, 1940-1941), 28, 35.

1164   Bass, Robert Duncan.   "The Plays and Playwrights of
       South Carolina. "   M. A.   University of South Caro-
       lina, Columbia, 1927.   66 p.   (18th cent. -)

1165   Watson, Charles Sullivan.   "Early Dramatic Writing
       in the South: Virginia and South Carolina Plays,
       1798-1830. "   Ph. D.   Vanderbilt University, 1966.
       335 p.   [67-04099]

       See also 1418, 1426, 1442.

SOUTH DAKOTA

BROOKINGS

1166   Switzer, Theodore R.   "A History of Theatre and
       Theatrical Activities in Brookings, South Dakota
       from 1879 through 1898. "   M. S. South Dakota
       State University, 1962.

1167   Arndt, Xavia Diane.   "A History of Theatre at South
       Dakota State University, 1892 through Summer,
       1972. "   M. A.   South Dakota State University, 1972.

DEADWOOD

1168   Naeseth, Henriette C. K.   "Drama in Early Deadwood,
       1869-1879. "   American Literature, 10 (November,
       1938), 289-312.

1169 Stine, Lawrence Carl. "A History of Theatre and
      Theatrical Activities in Deadwood, South Dakota,
      1876-90. " Ph. D. University of Iowa, 1962.
      513 p. [62-02411]

      See also 1452, 1453.

DELL RAPIDS

1170 Perrin, Gerry A. "A History of the Theatrical and
      Community Activities in the Early Dell Rapids,
      South Dakota, Opera House. " M. A. South Dakota
      State University, 1970.

MITCHELL

1171 Schilling, Katherine Tracy. "The History of Dramatic
      Art at Dakota Wesleyan University, 1885-1956. "
      M. A. University of South Dakota, 1957. 117 p.

SPEARFISH

1172 Farrell, Kenneth Lawrence. "A History of the Mat-
      thews Opera House and Repertory Theatre in Spear-
      fish, South Dakota From 1886 to 1930. " M. S. Uni-
      versity of Oregon, 1963. 188 p. [M-559]

VERMILLION

1173 Collins, Betty Jean. "History of Dramatic Art at the
      University of South Dakota from 1882-1947. " M. A.
      University of South Dakota, 1948.

YANKTON

1174 Koch, John C. "Yankton Theatre (Trading Posts to
      Opera House--1865-1900). " M. A. University of
      South Dakota, 1971. 258 p.

      See also 1447.

TENNESSEE

CHATTANOOGA

1175 Jones, Marian Porcher. "Some Notes for a History
      of the Chattanooga Theatre, 1877-1888. " M. A.
      Duke University, 1942.

JOHNSON CITY

1176 Daniels, Ophelia Cope. "The Formative Years of
      Johnson City, Tennessee, 1885-1900. " M. A. Ten-
      nessee State University, 1948.

MEMPHIS

1777 Ritter, Charles Clifford. "The Theater in Memphis,
      Tennessee, From Its Beginning to 1859. " Ph. D.
      University of Iowa, 1956. 393 p. [00-17484]
      (1829-)

1178 _____. " 'The Drama in Our Midst'--The Early
      History of the Theater in Memphis. " West Ten-
      nessee Historical Society Papers, 11 (1957), 5-35.
      (1829-1859)

1179 Luttrell, Wanda Melvina. "The Theatre of Memphis,
      Tennessee, From 1829 to 1860. " M. A. Louisiana
      State University, 1951.

1180 Chisman, Margaret Sue. "Literature and the Drama
      in Memphis, Tennessee, to 1860. " M. A. Duke
      University, 1942. (1829-)

1181 Hill, Raymond S. "Memphis Theatre, 1836-1846. "
      West Tennessee Historical Society Papers, 9 (1955),
      48-58.

1182 Edwall, Harry R. "The Golden Era of Minstrelsy in
      Memphis: A Reconstruction. " West Tennessee
      Historical Society Papers, 9 (1955), 29-47. (1843-
      1860)

1183 Faulkner, Seldon. "The New Memphis Theater of
      Memphis, Tennessee, From 1859 to 1880. " Ph. D.
      University of Iowa, 1957. 296 p. [00-22079]

1184 Bristow, Eugene Kerr. " 'Look Out for Saturday
      Night': A Social History of Professional Variety
      Theater in Memphis, Tennessee, 1859-1880. " Ph. D.
      University of Iowa, 1956. 227 p. [00-18522]

1185 _____. "Variety Theatre in Memphis, 1859-1862. "
      West Tennessee Historical Society Papers, 13
      (1959), 117-127.

1186 _____. "The Low Varieties Program in Memphis,
      1865-1873. " Quarterly Journal of Speech, 44 (De-
      cember, 1958), 423-427.

1187 _____. "Charley Broom, Variety Manager in Mem-
      phis, Tennessee, 1866-1872. " Southern Speech
      Quarterly, 25 (Fall, 1959), 11-20.

1188 Powell, Carolyn. "The Lyceum Theater of Memphis,
      1890-1900. " M. A. University of Mississippi, 1951.

1189 Young, John P. Standard History of Memphis, Ten-
      nessee. Knoxville, Tennessee, 1912. pp. 470-
      475.

NASHVILLE

1190 Morrow, Sara Sprott. "A Brief History of Theater
      in Nashville, 1807-1970. " Tennessee Historical
      Quarterly, 30 (Summer, 1971), 178-189.

1191 Hunt, Douglas Lucas. "The Nashville Theatre, 1830-
      1840. " Birmingham-Southern College Bulletin, 28
      (May, 1935), 1-89.

1192 Davenport, Francis Garvin. Cultural Life in Nash-
      ville on the Eve of the Civil War. Chapel Hill:
      University of North Carolina Press, 1941. Chap-
      ters 5 & 6. (1850-1860)

1193 Brockett, Oscar G. "Theatre in Nashville During the
      Civil War. " Southern Speech Journal, 23 (Winter,
      1957), 61-72. (1861-1865)

1194 Holding, Charles E. "John Wilkes Booth Stars in
      Nashville. " Tennessee Historical Quarterly, 23
      (March, 1964), 73-79. (1864)

1195 Stevens, Eva Cruzen. "The History of the Theatre
      in Nashville, Tennessee, 1871-1875. " M. A. Van-
      derbilt University, 1934.

1196 Maiden, Lewis Smith. "A Chronicle of the Theater in
      Nashville, Tennessee, 1876-1900. " Ph. D. Vander-
      bilt University, 1955. 817 p. [00-13755]

1197 _____. "The Theatre in Nashville, 1876-1900. "
      Southern Speech Journal, 29 (Fall, 1963), 20-25.

1198 _____. "Three Theatrical Stars in Nashville, 1876-
      1906. " Southern Speech Journal, 31 (Summer, 1966),
      338-347.

1199 Lewis, Meriwether L. (Series of articles on theatri-
      cal history of Nashville), Nashville Banner, Oc-
      tober 1, 8, 15, 22; November 5, 12, 19, 26; De-
      cember 3, 17, 24, 31, 1933.

      See also 932.

TEXAS

AMARILLO

1200 Phelps, LaVerne P. "History of the Little Theater
      Movement in Amarillo, Texas, from 1888 to
      1946. " M. A. West Texas State University, 1946.

AUSTIN

1201 Petmecky, Bill. "Millett and Hancock Opera Houses. "
      Junior Historian, 19 (January, 1959), 31-32.
      (1878, 1896)

      See also 1242.

COMMERCE

1202 Westhafer, Steven James. "A History of Drama at
      East Texas State University, 1889-1967. " M. S.
      East Texas State University, 1967.

CORSICANA

1203 Braden, Edwina Coltharp. "A History of Theatre in
      Corsicana, Texas, 1875 to 1915. " M. S. East
      Texas State University, 1969.

DALLAS

1204 "Theatrical History of Fort Worth, Dallas. " Bohemian,
      3 (1901-1902), 67-71.

1205 Adair, W. S. "Variety Theatres Flourished in Early
      Days in Dallas. " Dallas News, March 27, 1921,
      p. 10.

1206 Rosenfield, John. (Article on history of theater in
      "50th Anniversary Edition"). Dallas Morning News,
      October 1, 1935.

EL PASO

1207 Brady, Donald Vincent. "History of El Paso Theatre:
      1881 to 1905. " Ph. D. Tulane University, 1965.
      400 p. [66-01544]

1208   . The Theatre in Early El Paso, 1881-1905.
      El Paso: Texas Western College Press, 1966. 39
      p. Southwestern Studies, Vol. 4, No. 1.

1209 Levy, Estelle Goodman. "El Paso Defends Her Cul-
      ture--Opera at the Pass of the North. " Password,
      4 (July, 1959), 90-95. (1884-1907)

1210   . "The Myra Opera House and Other Theaters
      in Old El Paso. " Password, 5 (April, 1960), 65-
      73. (1884-)

FORT WORTH

1211 Megarity, Shirley Ann. "The Theatre in Fort Worth,
      1870-1899. " M. A. Texas Woman's University,
      1971. 96 p.

1212   Priddy, Billy. "Progress of the Theater in Fort
       Worth. " Junior Historian, 14 (December, 1953),
       19-20, 28. (1870-1953)

1213   Plasters, Warren Howard. "A History of Amusements
       in Forth Worth from the Beginning to 1879. " M. A.
       Texas Christian University, 1947. 62 p.

1214   Lane, Doris Ann. "A History of the Fort Worth The-
       ater from 1880 to 1888. " M. A. Texas Christian
       University, 1948. 99 p.

1215   Shannon, Hallie D. "The Theater in Fort Worth from
       1892 to 1896. " M. A. Texas Christian University,
       1950. 128 p.

1216   Walsh, Alice W. "The Theater in Fort Worth from
       1896 to 1900. " M. A. Texas Christian University,
       1952. 125 p.

1217   "Theatrical History of Fort Worth, Dallas. " Bohemian,
       3 (1901-1902), 67-71.

GALVESTON

1218   Gallegly, Joseph S. Footlights on the Border: The
       Galveston and Houston Stage Before 1900. The
       Hague: Mouton & Co. , 1962. 262 p. (1839-)

1219   _____. "The Renaissance of the Galveston The-
       atre: Henry Greenwall's First Season, 1867-1868. "
       Southwestern Historical Quarterly, 62 (April,
       1959), 442-456.

1220   _____. "The Tremont Opera House of Galveston:
       The First Years. " Rice Institute Pamphlet, 45
       (January, 1959), 52-70. (1871-1872)

1221   _____. "Edwin Booth in Galveston and Houston. "
       Rice Institute Pamphlet, 44 (April, 1957), 52-64.
       (1881, 1887, 1888)

GREENVILLE

1222   Price, Joyce Dyer. "A History of the King Opera
       House in Greenville, Texas. " M. A. East Texas
       State University, 1967. (1890-1934)

HOUSTON

1223   Yocum, Jack Harlan. "A History of the Theatre in
       Houston, 1836-1954. " Ph. D. University of Wis-
       consin, Madison, 1955. 2 vols. iv, 611 p.

1224   Broughton, Caroline. "Houston Theaters, Past and
       Present. " Junior Historian, 20 (September, 1959),
       18-21. (1836-1944)

1225   _____. "Houston Theatres, Past and Present. "
       Junior Historian, 19 (1958), 23-26, 30.

1226   Gallegly, Joseph S. Footlights on the Border: The
       Galveston and Houston Stage Before 1900. The
       Hague: Mouton & Co. , 1962. 262 p. (1838-)

1227   Fletcher, Edward Garland. The Beginnings of the
       Professional Theatre in Texas. Austin, Texas:
       The University, 1936. 55 p. University of Texas
       Bulletin, No. 3621, (June 1, 1936). (1838-1841)

1228   Muir, Andrew Forest, ed. "Diary of a Young Man in
       Houston, 1838. " Southwestern Historical Quarterly,
       53 (January, 1950), 276-307.

1229   Gallegly, Joseph S. "Plays and Players at Pillot's
       Opera House. " Southwestern Historical Quarterly,
       66 (July, 1962), 43-58. (1879-1889)

1230   _____. "Edwin Booth in Galveston and Houston. "
       Rice Institute Pamphlet, 44 (April, 1957), 52-64.
       (1881, 1887, 1888)

1231   "Theatrical Great Have Trod Local Boards. " Houston
       Chronicle, anniversary number, February 22, 1938.

JACKSONVILLE

1232   Acker, Will Hill. "History of the Theatrical Activities
       at Lou Morris College, Jacksonville, Texas, from
       September, 1873 to September, 1942. " M. A.
       Southern Methodist University, 1954.

JEFFERSON

       See 1253.

LONGVIEW

See 1253.

MARSHALL

1233 Groves, William McDonald, Jr. "A History of the
      Professional Theatre in Marshall, Texas, From
      1877 to 1915. " M. A. Stephen F. Austin State Uni-
      versity, 1976. 156 p. [1309255]

      See also 1242, 1253.

PITTSBURG

See 1253.

SAN ANTONIO

1234 Brokow, John W. "A Mexican-American Acting Com-
      pany, 1849-1924. " Educational Theatre Journal,
      27 (March, 1975), 23-29.

1235 Myler, Charles Bennett. "History of the English-
      Speaking Theatre in San Antonio Before 1900. "
      Ph. D. University of Texas, 1968. 370 p. [68-
      16120] (1851-)

1236 Chesnut, Glenn F. "The Drama in San Antonio, Tex-
      as From 1884 to 1889. " M. A. St. Mary's Uni-
      versity, 1949.

1237 Carroll, Vernon Hillion. "An Analysis of Theatrical
      Criticisms of Plays Presented in the Grand Opera
      House, San Antonio, Texas, 1886-1896, Excluding
      Operas, Operettas, and Variety Shows. " M. A.
      Southwest Texas State University, 1972.

1238 Stone, Delza H. "Drama in San Antonio, 1889-1894. "
      M. A. St. Mary's University, San Antonio, 1944.

TEXARKANA

1239 Clark, Linda Kidd. "A Theater History of Texarkana
      from 1876 through 1924. " M. S. East Texas State
      University, 1972.

      See also 1253.

TERRELL

1240   Hardin, Wylie Audrain. "A History of Theatre in
       Terrell, Texas, from 1890 through 1910. " M. S.
       East Texas State University, 1971.

WACO

1241   Shank, Phillip J. "A History of the Early Variety
       Theatres and Legitimate Theatres in Waco, Texas,
       From the Beginnings to 1928. " M. A. Baylor Uni-
       versity, 1977.

GENERAL

1242   King, Clyde Richard. "A History of the Theater in
       Texas, 1722-1900. " Ph. D. Baylor University,
       1962. 509 p.

1243   Hogan, William Ransom. "The Theatre in the Re-
       public of Texas. " Southwest Review, 19 (July,
       1934), 374-401. (1838-1846)

1244   _____. The Texas Republic: A Social and Eco-
       nomic History. Norman: University of Oklahoma
       Press, 1946.

1245   Holden, William Curry. "Frontier Problems and
       Movements in West Texas, 1846-1900. " Ph. D.
       University of Texas, 1927. Chapter 9, "Amuse-
       ments, " pp. 307-347.

1246   Hoole, William Stanley. "Simms' Michael Bonham--A
       'Forgotten' Drama of the Texas Revolution. "
       Southwestern Historical Quarterly, 46 (January,
       1943), 255-262. (1852)

1247   Spell, Lota M. "The Theatre in Texas Before the
       Civil War. " The Texas Monthly, 5 (April, 1930),
       291-301.

1248   King, C. Richard. "Texas' Theatrical Impresario. "
       East Texas Historical Journal, 4 (October, 1966),
       128-139.

1249   Hastings, Catherine Troxell. "The Historical Devel-
       opment of Fine Arts in Texas. " M. A. North Texas
       State University, 1949.

1250   Hunter, John Marvin, Sr.   ''Mollie Bailey, Great
       Showwoman. '' Frontier Times, 27 (April, 1950),
       183-193. (1866-1918)

1251   Carrow, Catherine Ikard.   ''The Amusements of Texas
       from 1880-1890. '' M. A. University of Texas,
       Austin, 1943.

1252   _____. ''Amusements for Men and Women in Texas
       in the 1880's. '' West Texas Historical Association
       Year Book, 23 (1947), 77-106.

1253   Reeves, Ann. ''Nineteenth Century Theatre in North-
       east Texas. '' M. F. A. University of Texas, Austin,
       1962. (Jefferson, Longview, Marshall, Pittsburg,
       Texarkana) (1875-1900)

       See also 850.

UTAH

BEAVER

       See 1287.

BRIGHAM CITY

1254   Johnson, Rue Corbett. ''A History of Drama in Co-
       rinne and Brigham City, Utah, 1855-1905. '' M. A.
       Brigham Young University, 1954.

1255   _____. ''Theatre in Zion: The Brigham City Dra-
       matic Association. '' Utah Historical Quarterly, 33
       (Summer, 1965), 187-197. (1855-1889)

CASTLE VALLEY

1256   Geary, Elmo G. ''A Study of Dramatics in Castle
       Valley from 1875 to 1925. '' M. S. University of
       Utah, 1953.

CEDAR CITY

See 1287.

CORINNE

1257 Johnson, Rue Corbett. "A History of Drama in Corinne and Brigham City, Utah, 1855-1905. " M. A.
Brigham Young University, 1954.

1258 _____ . "Frontier Theatre: The Corinne Opera
House. " Utah Historical Quarterly, 42 (Summer,
1974), 285-295. (1870-1890's)

LOGAN

1259 Brewer, Courtney H. "A History of Drama in Logan,
Utah, and Neighboring Communities to 1925. "
Ph. D. Brigham Young University, 1972. 449 p.
[72-22365] (1879-)

OGDEN

1260 Oaks, Harold Rasmas. "An Evaluation of the Beginnings, Purposes, and Influence of Drama in Ogden
from 1840 to 1900. " M. A. Brigham Young University, 1962.

1261 Browning, Beth. "History of Drama in Odgen. " M. A.
Brigham Young University, 1947. (1847-1947)

PAROWAN

1262 Mitchell, Albert Orton. "Pioneers and Players of
Parowan. " Utah Humanities Review, 1 (January,
1947), 38-52. (1850-1859)

See also 1287.

PROVO

1263 Olauson, Clarence Ronald. "Dramatic Activities at
the Brigham Young University from the Earliest
Beginnings to the Present, 1849-1961. " M. F. A.
University of Utah, 1962.

1264 Ferguson, Burnett B. "History of Drama in Provo, Utah,
1853-1897. " M. A. Brigham Young University, 1952.

ST. GEORGE

See 1287.

SALT LAKE CITY

1265 Henderson, Myrtle Elizabeth. "A History of the The-
      atre in Salt Lake City to 1870. " M. S. North-
      western University, 1935. (1840's-)

1266 _____. A History of the Theatre in Salt Lake City
      from 1850 to 1870. Evanston, Illinois, 1934. Salt
      Lake City: Deseret Book Company, 1941.

1267 Evans, Edmund Emil. "An Historical Study of the
      Drama of the Latter Day Saints. " Ph. D. Univer-
      sity of Southern California, 1941. 3 vols. 672 p.
      (1850-1878)

1268 Roylance, Aaron Alma. "The Salt Lake Theatre As
      An Organizational Unit. " Ph. D. University of
      Utah, 1963. viii, 186 p. [64-03149] (1850-1928)

1269 Margetts, Winifred Snell. "A Study of the Salt Lake
      City Actor from 1850 to 1869. " M. A. University
      of Utah, 1948.

1270 Pyper, George Dollinger. Romance of an Old Play-
      house. Salt Lake City: Seagull Press, 1928.
      343 p. (1850-)

1271 Alexander, Sara. "Recollections of the Mormon The-
      atre. " Dramatic Magazine, 1 (August, 1880), 312-
      316. (1861-)

1272 Todd, Therald Francis. "The Operation of the Salt
      Lake Theatre, 1862-1875. " Ph. D. University of
      Oregon, 1973. vi, 292 p. [74-06907]

1273 Nelson, George-Merwin. "A Pioneer Playhouse. "
      The Theatre, 23 (January, 1916), 34-36. (1862-)

1274 Leigh, Ora V. "The Stage on Which Maude Adams
      First Appeared. " The Theatre, 9 (March, 1909),
      88, 90-91. (1862-)

1275 White, Matthew, Jr. "Where Maude Adams Began. "
      Munsey's Magazine, 46 (1912), 898-899.

1276 Pardoe, T. Earl. "The Salt Lake Theatre in the
      Sixties. " Drama, 19 (January, 1929), 106. (1862)

1277 Russell, Isaac. "A Pioneer Municipal Theatre and Its
      Lesson. " Craftsman, 19 (1911), 563-568.

1278 Lambourne, Alfred. "Reminiscences of the Salt Lake
      Theatre. " Improvement Era, 15 (1912), 529-541,
      696-702.

1279 _____. Play-House ... With Glimpses of the Pio-
      neers and a Few Notables. Salt Lake City: n. p. ,
      191?. 64 p.

1280 Whitney, Horace G. The Drama in Utah: The Story
      of the Salt Lake Theatre. Salt Lake City: Deseret
      News, 1915. 48 p. From Improvement Era, 18
      (1915), 509-516, 580-592, 686-695, 790-804.

1281 Engar, Keith Maurice. "History of Dramatics at the
      University of Utah from Beginning until June, 1919. "
      M. F. A. University of Utah, 1948.

GENERAL

1282 Hansen, Harold Ivan. "A History and Influence of the
      Mormon Theatre from 1839-1869. " Ph. D. Uni-
      versity of Iowa, 1949. 205 p.

1283 Gledhill, Preston Ray. "Mormon Dramatic Activities. "
      Ph. D. University of Wisconsin, Madison, 1950.
      vii, 396 p. (1839-1950)

1284 Monson, Leland Hans. "Shakespeare in Utah (1847-
      1900). " Ph. D. University of Utah, 1956. vii,
      308 p. [00-17574]

1285 _____. "Shakespeare in Early Utah. " Improvement
      Era, 63 (October, 1960), 718-721, 763-764. (1847-
      1900)

1286 Robertson, Roderick. "The Early Mormon Theatre. "
      Quarterly Journal of Speech, 44 (February, 1958),
      40-49. (1850-1863)

1287 Mitchell, Albert Orton. "Dramatics in Southern Utah--
      Parowan, Cedar City, Beaver, St. George--from

1850 to the Coming of the Moving Pictures. " M. A. University of Utah, 1935.

1288 Maughan, Ila Fisher. "History of Staging and Business Methods of the Deseret Dramatic Association, 1852-1869. " M. A. University of Utah, 1949. 276 p.

1289 Lindsay, John Shanks. The Mormons and the Theatre: Or, The History of Theatricals in Utah, With Reminiscences and Comments, Humorous and Critical. Salt Lake City: Century Printing, 1905. 178 p.

1290 Thorpe, William H. "The Mormons and the Drama. " M. A. Columbia University, 1921.

1291 Carter, Kate B. "History of Drama in the West. " Heart Throbs of the West, Vol. 4. Salt Lake City, 1943, pp. 77-116.

1292 Adams, Allen John. "Peter McCourt, Jr. and the Silver Theatrical Circuit, 1889-1910: An Historical and Biographical Study. " Ph. D. University of Utah, 1969. viii, 267 p. [70-02020]

See also 799, 1451, 1456.

VERMONT

BURLINGTON

1293 Taft, R. S. "The Theatre in Burlington in 1808, and a Whitehall Dinner. " Vermont Antiquarian Society Proceedings and Papers, 1 (1901), 75-85.

1294 Bryan, George B. "The Howard Opera House in Burlington. " Vermont History, 45 (Fall, 1977), 197-220.

GENERAL

1295 Dell, Robert M. , and Charles A. Huguenin. "Ver-

mont's Royall Tyler in New York's John Street
Theatre: A Theatrical Hoax Exploded. " Vermont
History, 38 (Spring, 1970), 103-112. (1787-1798)

VIRGINIA

ALEXANDRIA

See 1343.

CHARLOTTESVILLE

1296   Waddell, Richard E. "Theatre in Charlottesville,
       1886-1912: The Levy Opera House and the Jeffer-
       son Auditorium. " M. A. University of Virginia,
       1972.

1297   . "The Theatre in Charlottesville: The Town
       Hall, The Levy Opera House and the Jefferson
       Auditorium. " Magazine of Albemarle County His-
       tory, 31 (1973), 11-30.

DUMFRIES

See 1341.

FREDERICKSBURG

See 1341, 1343.

LYNCHBURG

1298   Hadley, Richard Hanna. "The Theatre in Lynchburg,
       Virginia, from Its Beginnings in 1822 to the Out-
       break of the Civil War. " Ph. D. University of
       Michigan, Ann Arbor, 1942. iii, 323 p.

NORFOLK

1299   Rowland, Thomas B. 'Norfolk Theatres of the Olden
       Times. " Lower Norfolk County Virginia Antiquary,
       2 (1898), 102.

1300 Tucker, George H. "Early Norfolk Theatres." Virginia Pilot, June 30, July 7 and 14, 1940.

See also 1336, 1341, 1343, 1345.

PETERSBURG

1301 Wyatt, Edward A., IV. "Three Petersburg Theaters."
William and Mary College Quarterly, Second Series,
21 (April, 1941), 83-110. (1751-1865)

See also 1336, 1341, 1343.

RICHMOND

1302 Shockley, Martin Staples. "The Richmond Theatre,
1780-1790." Virginia Magazine of History and
Biography, 60 (July, 1952), 421-436.

1303 _____. The Richmond Stage, 1784-1812. Charlottesville: University Press of Virginia, 1977. 451 p.

1304 _____. "First American Performances of English
Plays in Richmond Before 1819." Journal of
Southern History, 13 (February, 1947), 91-105.
(1790-)

1305 Joynes, Thomas R. "The Burning of the Richmond
Theatre, 1811." Virginia Magazine of History and
Biography, 51 (July, 1943), 297-300.

1306 Gaines, William H., Jr. "The Fatal Lamp, or Panic
at the Play, as Performed at the Theater in Richmond on the Night of December 26, 1811." Virginia Cavalcade, 2 (Summer, 1952), 4-8.

1307 Shockley, Martin Staples. "A History of the Theatre
in Richmond, Virginia, 1819-1838." Ph. D. University of North Carolina, Chapel Hill, 1938. 2 vols.
610 p.

1308 _____. "American Plays in the Richmond Theatre,
1819-1838." Studies in Philology, 37 (January,
1940), 100-119.

1309 _____. "Shakspere's Plays in the Richmond Theatre, 1819-1838." Shakespeare Association Bulletin, 15 (April, 1940), 88-94.

1310 _____. "The Proprietors of Richmond's New The-
      atre of 1819." William and Mary Quarterly, Sec-
      ond Series, 19 (July, 1939), 302-308. (1819-1838)

1311 Cate, Wirt Armistead. "Ford, the Booths, and Lin-
      coln's Assassination." Emory University Quarterly,
      5 (March, 1949), 11-19. (1821-1865)

1312 Shockley, Martin Staples. "First American Perform-
      ances of Some English Plays." Elizabethan Studies
      and Other Essays in Honor of George F. Reynolds.
      Boulder: University of Colorado Press, 1945.
      University of Colorado Studies, Series B, Vol. 2,
      No. 4, pp. 302-306. (1822-1838)

1313 _____. "Priscilla Cooper in the Richmond The-
      atre." Virginia Magazine of History and Biography,
      67 (April, 1959), 180-185. (1836-1838)

1314 Fuller, Charles F., Jr. "Kunkel and Company at the
      Marshall Theatre, Richmond, Virginia, 1856-1861."
      M. F. A. Ohio University, 1968.

1315 _____. "Edwin and John Wilkes Booth, Actors at
      the Old Marshall Theatre in Richmond." Virginia
      Magazine of History and Biography, 79 (October,
      1971), 477-483. (1856-1859)

1316 Harwell, Richard Barksdale. "Civil War Theater:
      The Richmond Stage." Civil War History, 1 (Sep-
      tember, 1955), 295-304. (1861-1865)

1317 _____. "Brief Candle: The Confederate Theatre."
      Proceedings of the American Antiquarian Society,
      81 (April, 1971), 41-160. (1861-1865)

1318 Theodore, Terry. "The Confederate Theatre: Rich-
      mond: Theatre Capitol of the Confederacy." Lin-
      coln Herald, 77 (Fall, 1975), 158-167.

1319 Waal, Carla. "The First Original Confederate Drama:
      The Guerrillas." Virginia Magazine of History and
      Biography, 70 (October, 1962), 459-467. (1862)

1320 Legg, Ruth R. "The New Richmond Theatre." M. A.
      Pennsylvania State University, 1963. (1885-1913)

1321 Chesterman, Bruce. "Walls of Historic Playhouse
      Preserved..." Richmond News Leader, October
      12, 1936.

      See also 1343, 1345, 1408, 1427, 1432.

TAPPAHANNOCK (HOBBS' HOLE)

      See 1336, 1341.

WILLIAMSBURG

1322 Simpson, Sister Mary Pius. "The Williamsburg The-
      atre, 1716-1774." M. A. Catholic University of
      America, 1948.

1323 Land, Robert H. "The First Williamsburg Theater."
      William and Mary Quarterly, Third Series, 5
      (July, 1948), 359-374. (1716-1745)

1324 "First Playhouse in Williamsburg." William and Mary
      College Quarterly, First Series, 24 (July, 1915),
      29-30. (1745)

1325 Nielsen, Mark Steven. "A Study of the Hallam Com-
      pany's Premier Production in Williamsburg, The
      Merchant of Venice." M. A. University of North
      Carolina, Chapel Hill, 1974. (1752)

1326 Tyler, Lyon G. Williamsburg, the Old Colonial Cap-
      itol. Richmond: Whittet and Shepperson, 1907.

1327 Ford, Paul L. Washington and The Theatre. New
      York: Dunlap Society, 1899. 68 p.

1328 Ragland, Herbert S. "Archaeological Report: Foun-
      dations of the First Theatre in America, Williams-
      burg, Virginia." Report to the Dept. of Research
      and Record, Colonial Williamsburg, Inc., May,
      1931.

1329 Stephenson, Mary A. "The First Theatre." Colonial
      Williamsburg, Department of Research, Ms Re-
      port, 1946.

1330 _____. "The Second Theatre." Colonial Williams-
      burg, Department of Research, Ms Report, 1946.

1331 Knight, James. "Archaeological Report, Block 29,
      Area G (Northwest Corner of Colonial Lot 164)."
      Report to the Dept. of Research and Record, Colo-
      nial Williamsburg, Inc., October, 1947.

1332 Moorehead, Singleton P. "The First Theatre and Its
      Site, A Summary of Facts Including Evidence."
      Report to the Dept. of Research and Record, Colo-
      nial Williamsburg, Inc., December, 1947.

1333 McNamara, Brooks. "Colonial Theatre Architecture."
      Colonial Williamsburg, Department of Research,
      Ms Report, 1965.

1334 "America's First Theatre." Richmond Times-Dis-
      patch, April 17, 1910, Sec. B, p. 6, col. 1-5.

      See also 1336, 1345, 1407, 1408, 1411.

GENERAL

1335 Bruce, Philip Alexander. "An Early Virginia Play."
      Nation, 88 (February 11, 1909), 136. (1665)

1336 Jones, Vernon A. "The Theatre in Colonial Virginia."
      Reviewer, 5 (January, 1925), 81-88. (Norfolk,
      Petersburg, Tappahannock, Williamsburg) (1665-
      1771)

1337 Land, Robert Hunt. "Theatre in Colonial Virginia."
      M.A. University of Virginia, 1936. 135 p. (1665-
      1770's)

1338 Barnes, James F., Jr. "Discovery of Old Daguerreo-
      type Establishes Place of Presentation of Ye Bare
      and Ye Cub." William & Mary Literary Magazine,
      33, No. 2 (n.d.), 118-119.

1339 Little, Paul Judson. "Reactions to the Theatre: Vir-
      ginia, Massachusetts, and Pennsylvania, 1665-
      1793." Ph.D. Syracuse University, 1969. 212 p.
      [70-12789]

1340 "America's First Theatre." Richmond Times-Dis-
      patch, April 17, 1910.

1341 H., F. "The Theatre in Eighteenth Century Virginia
      Outside of Williamsburg." Virginia Magazine of

History and Biography, 35 (July, 1927), 295-296.
(Dumfries, Fredericksburg, Norfolk, Petersburg,
Hobbs' Hole)   (1751-1752)

1342   Rankin, Hugh F.   "Virginia and the Colonial Theatre. "
       Arts in Virginia, 1 (1961), 22-29.

1343   Sherman, Susanne Ketchum.   "Post-Revolutionary The-
       atre in Virginia, 1784-1810. " M. A. The College
       of William and Mary, 1950. (Alexandria, Freder-
       icksburg, Norfolk, Petersburg, Richmond)

1344   Watson, Charles Sullivan.   "Early Dramatic Writing
       in the South: Virginia and South Carolina Plays,
       1798-1830. " Ph. D. Vanderbilt University, 1966.
       ii, 332 p. [67-04099]

1345   Sherman, Susanne K.   "Thomas Wade West, Thea-
       trical Impresario, 1790-1799. " William and Mary
       Quarterly, Third Series, 9 (January, 1952), 10-28.
       (Norfolk, Richmond, Williamsburg)

       See also 1398, 1426, 1442.

WASHINGTON

OLYMPIA

       See 1362.

SEATTLE

1346   Grant, Howard Franklin.   The Story of Seattle's Early
       Theatres.   Seattle: University of Washington Book-
       store, 1934.   47 p.   (1852-1900)

1347   Sayre, James Willis.   "A List of All Plays Given in
       Seattle from the Beginning to Date. " Ms. , Seattle
       Public Library.   207 p.

1348   _____.   "A Complete Record of Places of Thea-
       trical Entertainment in Seattle From the Beginning
       to Date. " Ms. , Seattle Public Library.   30 p.

1349   _____. "Players Who Have Appeared in Seattle. "
        Ms, Seattle Public Library.   197 p.

1350   Elliott, Eugene Clinton.   A History of Variety-Vaude-
        ville in Seattle from the Beginning to 1914.   Se-
        attle: University of Washington Press, 1944.   84
        p. (1852-)

1351   Ladd, James William.   "A Survey of the Legitimate
        Theatre in Seattle Since 1856. "   M. A. Washington
        State University, 1935.   (-1910)

1352   Sayre, J. Willis.   "Complete Bookings at All Seattle
        Playhouses from the Beginning to Date (1863-1948). "
        Ms. , Seattle Public Library.   538 p.

1353   Grant, Ethel Austin.   Theatrical Performances in Yes-
        ler's Hall, 1865-1867, in Squire's Opera House,
        1879-1882, and in the Standard Theatre, Seattle;
        And a Preferatory List of Places of Theatrical En-
        tertainments in Seattle by J. Willis Sayre.   Seattle:
        University of Washington, 1939.   98 p.

1354   Nelson, Edwin L.   "A History of Road Shows in Se-
        attle, from Their Beginnings to 1914. "   M. A. Uni-
        versity of Washington, 1947.   (1869-)

1355   Elliott, Eugene Clinton.   "History of Variety Vaude-
        ville in Seattle from the Beginning to 1914. "   M. A.
        University of Washington, 1941.   (1870-)

1356   Walker, Phillip Nathaniel.   "A History of Dramatics
        at the University of Washington from the Beginning
        to June, 1919. "   M. A. University of Washington,
        1947.   (1875-)

1357   Rohrer, Mary Katherine.   "The History of Seattle
        Stock Companies from Their Beginnings to 1934. "
        M. A. University of Washington, 1939.   (1890-)

1358   _____.   The History of Seattle Stock Companies
        from Their Beginnings to 1934.   Seattle: Uni-
        versity of Washington Press, 1945.   76 p. (1890-)

1359   Tarrach, Dean Arthur.   "Alexander Pantages: The
        Seattle Pantages and His Vaudeville Circuit. "   M. A.
        University of Washington, 1973.   (1897-1940)

See also 1362, 1452.

SPOKANE

1360 Reams, Danny I. "Spokane Theatre, 1880 to 1892."
      M. A. Washington State University, 1970.

1361 Wasserman, Bruce Martin. "Early Theatre in Spokane,
      Washington, 1889-1902." Ph. D. Washington State
      University, 1975. vii, 438 p. [75-16194]

      See also 1362.

TACOMA

      See 1362.

WALLA WALLA

      See 1362, 1457.

GENERAL

1362 Berelson, Bernard, and Howard F. Grant. "The
      Pioneer Theatre in Washington." Pacific North-
      west Quarterly, 28 (April, 1937), 115-136. (Olym-
      pia, Seattle, Spokane, Tacoma, Walla Walla)
      (1852-)

1363 Sayre, James Willis. "A Half Century of Cultural
      Progress: Theatre." Ed. Charles Miles and O. B.
      Sperlin. Building a State, Washington, 1889-1939.
      Tacoma: Pionner, Inc., 1940. pp. 184-188.

      See also 1451, 1454.

WEST VIRGINIA

CHARLESTON

1364 Radow, Rhoda Kirschner. "A History of the Burlew
      Opera House, Charleston, West Virginia from 1891-
      1920." M. A. Marshall University, 1964.

1365 Gallant, Carol. "Theatres of the South: The Old Opera House of Charles Town, West Virginia. " Southern Theatre, 18 (Summer, 1975), 29-31.

HUNTINGTON

1366 Jones, Robin Adair. "A History of the Professional Legitimate Theatre in Huntington from 1871 to 1928. " M. A. Marshall University, 1957.

WHEELING

1367 Wingerter, Charles A. History of Greater Wheeling and Vicinity. Chicago & New York: Lewis Publ. Co. , 1912. Vol. 1, pp. 481-487.

WISCONSIN

EAU CLAIRE

1368 Wolfert, Wayne Richard. "Theatre in Eau Claire, Wisconsin: A History of the Grand Opera House (1883-1930). " Ph. D. University of Wisconsin, Madison, 1972. 2 vols. 915 p. [72-24916]

LA CROSSE

1369 Siefkas, James M. "A History of Theatre in La Crosse, Wisconsin, from Its Beginnings to 1900. " Ph. D. University of Missouri, Columbia, 1972. 206 p. [73-21828] (1858-)

MADISON

1370 Youngerman, Henry Clayman. "Theatrical Activities: Madison, Wisconsin, 1836-1907. " Ph. D. University of Wisconsin, 1940. 423 p.

1371 _____ . "Theater Buildings in Madison, Wisconsin, 1836-1900. " Wisconsin Magazine of History, 30 (March, 1947), 273-288.

1372 Mailer, Julia H. "Gala Nights and Gaslights. " Wisconsin Stage, 8 (Winter, 1954-1955), 5-7. (1890-)

1373 Stearns, Nancy Hoffmann. "Theatrical Activities of Madison, Wisconsin, 1899-1973. " M. A. University of Wisconsin, Madison, 1974. 207 p.

MENOMONIE

1374 Bousliman, Charles William. "The Mabel Tainter Memorial Theatre: A Pictorial Case Study of a Late Nineteenth-Century American Playhouse. " Ph. D. Ohio State University, 1969. xv, 276 p. [70-13984]

1375 Heagle, Lawrence. "The Cessation of Professional Theatre at the Mabel Tainter Theatre, Menomonie, Wisconsin: A Historical-Critical Analysis. " M. S. University of Wisconsin, Eau Claire, 1968. (1890-1940)

MILWAUKEE

1376 O'Shea, Joseph James. "A History of the English Speaking, Professional Stage in Milwaukee, Wisconsin, 1842-76. " Ph. D. Northwestern University, 1964. 6 vols. 2286 p. [65-03299]

1377 McDavitt, Elaine Elizabeth. "A History of the Theatre in Milwaukee, Wisconsin, from Its Beginnings to 1865. " M. A. Northwestern University, 1935.

1378 Bredlow, Lulu Elizabeth. "A History of the German Theatre of Milwaukee from 1850 to 1935. " M. A. Northwestern University, 1936.

1379 Kaiser, Norman James. "A History of the German Theater of Milwaukee from 1850 to 1890. " M. S. University of Wisconsin, Madison, 1954.

1380 Magyar, Francis. "The History of the Early Milwaukee German Theatre (1850-1868). " Wisconsin Magazine of History, 13 (June, 1930), 375-386.

1381 Herbatschek, Heinrich. "Die Anfänge des deutschen Theaters in Milwaukee. " American German Review, 13 (February, 1947), 17-18. (1850-1854)

1382 Andressohn, John C. "Die Literarische Geschichte des
      Milwaukeer Deutschen Buhnenwesens, 1850-1911. "
      German-American Annals, New Series 10 (1912),
      65-88, 150-170.

1383 Isaacs, Edith J. R. , and Rosamond Gilder. "The Ger-
      man Theatre in Milwaukee. " Theatre Arts, 28
      (August, 1944), 465-474.

1384 Lansing, P. B.   Diagrams of Milwaukee Theatres.
      Milwaukee: Burdick, Armitage & Allen, 1890.
      32 p.

1385 Monfried, Walter.   'Famous American Theatres. "
      Theatre Arts, 42 (April, 1958), 68-69. (1890-)

1386 Conard, Howard L.   "Theatres and Amusement Halls. "
      History of Milwaukee from Its First Settlement to
      the Year 1895. Chicago, 1895. Vol. 2, pp. 121-
      123.

OSHKOSH

      See 1471.

PORTAGE

1387 Ernsberger, Sam.   "Theatricals in the Old Days. "
      The Wisconsin Idea Theatre Quarterly, 6 (Summer,
      1952), 10-14. (1878-)

WHITEWATER

1388 Madsen, John A.   "A History of Theatre from March
      25, 1857 to October 2, 1900 in Whitewater, Wis-
      consin. " M. S. T. University of Wisconsin, White-
      water, 1971.

WYOMING

CHEYENNE

1389 Bell, William Campton.   "A History of the Theatrical

Activities of Cheyenne, Wyoming, from 1867 to
1902. "   M. A. Northwestern University, 1935.   2
vols.

1390 _____ . "The Early Theaters, Cheyenne, Wyoming,
1867-1882. " Annals of Wyoming, 25 (January,
1953), 3-21.

1391 "Do You Know That. " Annals of Wyoming, 14 (July,
1942), 179.   (1867)

See also 1447, 1452.

LARAMIE

1392 Kaiser, Louis H.   "A Theatrical History of Laramie,
Wyoming, 1868-1880. "   M. A. University of Wyoming, 1950.

1393 Boustkeon, Lindy.   "History of the Laramie Theatre
(1881-1890). "   M. A. University of Wyoming, 1961.

GENERAL

1394 Adams, Allen John.   "Peter McCourt, Jr. and the
Silver Theatrical Circuit, 1889-1910: An Historical
and Biographical Study. "   Ph. D. University of
Utah, 1969.   viii, 267 p.   [70-02020]

See also 1456.

EAST REGION

1395 Coad, Oral Sumner. "American Theatre in the 18th Century." South Atlantic Quarterly, 17 (July, 1918), 190-197. (1665-1798)

1396 Morgan, Edmund S. "Puritan Hostility to the Theatre." Proceedings of the American Philosophical Society, 110 (October, 1966), 340-347.

1397 Lovell, John, Jr. "The Beginnings of the American Theatre." Theatre Annual, 10 (1952), 7-19.

1398 Taylor, Joseph Richard. "Early American Drama." Bostonia, 6 (February, 1933), 3-6, 21-22; (March, 1933), 10-14. (Boston, New York, Virginia) (1702-1849)

1399 Coad, Oral Sumner. "Stage and Players in Eighteenth Century America." Journal of English and Germanic Philology, 19 (April, 1920), 201-223. (1703-1799)

1400 Rankin, Hugh Franklin. "The Colonial Theatre: Its History and Operations." Ph. D. University of North Carolina, Chapel Hill, 1960. 540 p. [60-04860]

1401 _____. The Theatre in Colonial America. Chapel Hill: University of North Carolina Press, 1965. 239 p.

1402 Ford, Paul Leicester. "The Beginnings of American Dramatic Literature." New England Magazine, New Series, 9 (February, 1894), 673-687. (1714-1789)

1403 McNamara, Brooks Barry. "The Development of the American Playhouse in the Eighteenth Century." Ph.D. Tulane University, 1965. 398 p. [66-01562]

1404 _____. The American Playhouse in the Eighteenth
          Century. Cambridge, Mass.: Harvard University
          Press, 1969. 174 p.

1405 Mates, Julian. "The American Musical Stage before
          1800." Ph. D. Columbia University, 1959. 356 p.
          [59-03118]

1406 _____. The American Musical Stage Before 1800.
          New Brunswick, New Jersey: Rutgers University
          Press, 1962. 298 p.

1407 Daley, Mary Patricia. "Journalistic Criticism of The-
          ater in Eighteenth Century America." Ph. D. Case
          Western Reserve University, 1976. v, 143 p.
          (Annapolis, Boston, Charleston, New York, Phila-
          delphia, Williamsburg) [76-28381] (1733-1800)

1408 Seilhamer, George Overcash. History of the American
          Theatre. 3 vols. Philadelphia: Globe Printing
          House, 1888-1891. (Albany, Annapolis, Baltimore,
          Boston, Charleston, Hartford, Newport, Philadel-
          phia, Portsmouth, Providence, Richmond, Salem,
          Savannah, Williamsburg) (1749-1797)

1409 Wolf, Edwin, II. "Colonial American Playbills."
          Pennsylvania Magazine of History and Biography,
          97 (January, 1973), 99-106. (1750-1773)

1410 McAneny, Marguerite. "Decorum and Delight, on
          Both Sides of the Footlights as Seen in the William
          Seymour Theatre Collection of the Princeton Uni-
          versity Library." Princeton University Library
          Chronicle, 27 (Spring, 1966), 167-181. (18th and
          19th century)

1411 McCosker, Susan. "The American Company, 1752-
          1791, Founders of the American Theatre." M. A.
          Catholic University of America, 1968. (Kingston,
          Philadelphia, Williamsburg)

1412 McNamara, Brooks Barry. "David Douglass and the
          Beginnings of American Theatre Architecture."
          Winterthur Portfolio, 3 (1967), 112-135. (1760)

1413 Wilmeth, Don B. "Cooke Among the Yankee Doodles."
          Theatre Survey, 14 (November, 1973), 1-32. (Bal-

timore, Boston, New York, Philadelphia, Providence) (1810-1812)

1414   Gafford, Lucile. "Transcendentalist Attitudes Towards Drama and the Theatre." New England Quarterly, 13 (1940), 442-466.

1415   Yeaton, Kelly. "New England Melodrama." The High School Thespian, 10 (March-April, 1939), 9, 20. (1875-1900)

1416   Cadby, Louise Kanazireff. "The History and Functioning of the Summer Theatre in New England." M. A. Hofstra University, 1967.

1417 Gay, Frederick. "The First American Play." Nation, 87 (February 11, 1909), 136.

1418 Sonneck, Oscar G. Early Opera in America. New York: G. Schirmer, 1915. (Maryland, South Carolina) (1735-1800)

1419 Utterback, Elizabeth. "History of the Development of Drama in the South." M. A. Peabody Institute, 1930.

1420 Pettit, Paul Bruce. "The Showboat Theatre: The Development of the Showboat on the Mississippi River and on the Eastern Waterways." M. A. Cornell University, 1943.

1421 Nolan, Paul T. "Drama in the Lower Mississippi States." Mississippi Quarterly, 19 (Winter, 1965-1966), 20-28. (Arkansas, Louisiana, Mississippi) (1814-1966)

1422 Dormon, James Hunter, Jr. "The Theatre in the Ante-Bellum South, 1815-1861." Ph. D. University of North Carolina, Chapel Hill, 1966. 544 p. [67-05334]

1423 _____. Theatre in the Ante-Bellum South 1815-1861. Chapel Hill: North Carolina University Press, 1967. 322 p.

1424 Graham, Philip. "Showboats in the South." Georgia Review, 12 (Summer, 1958), 174-185. (1831-)

1425 Yeomans, Gordon Allen. "The Contributions of William Henry Crisp to the Southern Ante-Bellum Theatre." M. A. Louisiana State University, 1952. (1850-1860)

1426 Fife, Iline. "The Theatre During the Confederacy. "
      Ph. D. Louisiana State University, 1949. (Alabama,
      Georgia, Louisiana, North Carolina, South Caro-
      lina, Virginia) (1861-1865)

1427 _____. "The Confederate Theatre. " Southern
      Speech Journal, 20 (Spring, 1955), 224-231. (Ma-
      con, New Orleans, Richmond, Savannah)

1428 Reardon, William R. "Civil War Theater: Formal
      Organization. " Civil War History, 1 (September,
      1955), 205-227.

1429 Brockett, Oscar G. , and Lenyth Brockett. "Civil War
      Theater: Contemporary Treatments. " Civil War
      History, 1 (September, 1955), 229-250.

1430 Welsh, Willard. "Civil War Theater: The War in
      Drama. " Civil War History, 1 (September, 1955),
      251-280.

1431 Reardon, William R. , and John Foxen. "Civil War
      Theater: The Propaganda Play. " Civil War His-
      tory, 1 (September, 1955), 281-293.

1432 Dannett, Sylvia G. L. "And the Show Went On ... In
      the Confederacy. " Maryland Historical Magazine,
      61 (June, 1966), 105-119. (Richmond, Wilmington)

1433 Theodore, Terry. "The Civil War on the New York
      Stage from 1861-1900: Civil War Figures on the
      New York Stage. " Lincoln Herald, 74 (Spring,
      1972), 34-40.

1434 _____. "The Civil War on the New York Stage
      from 1861-1900: Civil War Drama 1861-1865. "
      Lincoln Herald, 74 (Winter, 1972), 203-210.

1435 _____. "The Civil War on the New York Stage
      from 1861-1900: Civil War Drama 1865-1877. "
      Lincoln Herald, 75 (Spring, 1973), 29-34.

1436 _____. "Civil War Drama, 1878-1900. " Lincoln
      Herald, 75 (Fall, 1973), 115-122.

1437 _____. "The Confederate Theatre: Theatre Per-
      sonalities and Practices During the Confederacy. "
      Lincoln Herald, 76 (Winter, 1974), 187-195.

1438 _____. "The Confederate Theatre: The Confederate Drama. " <u>Lincoln Herald</u>, 77 (Spring, 1975), 33-41.

1439 _____. "The Confederate Theatre: Confederate Theatre in the Deep South. " <u>Lincoln Herald</u>, 77 (Summer, 1975), 102-114.

1440 _____. "The Confederate Theatre: Richmond: Theatre Capitol of the Confederacy. " <u>Lincoln Herald</u>, 77 (Fall, 1975), 158-167.

1441 DeLéry, Simone Rivière. "Sarah Bernhardt and the Deep South. " <u>French Review</u>, 27 (February, 1954), 269-274. (1881)

1442 Lanier, Doris. "Bill Nye in the South. " <u>Annals of Wyoming</u>, 46 (Fall, 1974), 253-262. (Georgia, South Carolina, Virginia) (1888-1889)

MIDWEST REGION

1443 Pettit, Paul Bruce. "Showboat Theatre." Quarterly
Journal of Speech, 31 (April, 1945), 167-175.
(1817-)

1444 Graham, Philip. Showboats: The History of an American Institution. Austin: University of Texas
Press, 1951. 224 p.

1445 Schick, Joseph S. "Early Showboat and Circus in the
Upper Valley." Mid-America, 32 (October, 1950),
211-225. (1833-1858)

1446 Briggs, Harold E., and Ernestine Bennett Briggs.
"The Early Theatre in the Upper Mississippi Valley." Mid-America, 31 (July, 1949), 131-162.
(Davenport, Des Moines, Dubuque, Galena, Minneapolis, St. Paul) (1834-1874)

1447 _____. "The Early Theatre on the Northern Plains."
Mississippi Valley Historical Review, 37 (Septem-
ber, 1950), 231-264. (Bismarck, Cheyenne, Fargo,
Fort Benton, Grand Forks, Miles City, Sioux City,
Yankton) (1867-1890's)

1448 Frenz, Horst. "The German Drama in the Middle
West." American-German Review, 8 (June, 1942),
15-17, 37. (1870's)

1449 McCormick, Walter James. "An Historical Study of
Showboat Theatre on the Missouri River." M.A.
Central Missouri State University, 1965.

1450 Latchaw, Truly Trousdale. "The Trousdale Brothers
Theatrical Companies from 1896 to 1915." M.A.
University of Minnesota, 1948.

163

1451 Baker, Donald Guy. "Shakespeare and the American
West. " M. A. Adams State College, 1969. (Cali-
fornia, Colorado, Nevada, North-Central Frontier,
The Pacific Northwest, Utah) (1845-1890)

1452 Briggs, Harold E. "Early Variety Theatres in the
Trans-Mississippi West. " Mid-America, 34 (July,
1952), 188-202. (Cheyenne, Deadwood, Denver,
Helena, San Francisco, Seattle, Tombstone, Tucson)
(1849-1892)

1453 Davis, Ronald L. "They Played for Gold: Theater on
the Mining Frontier. " Southwest Review, 51 (Spring,
1966), 169-184. (Central City, Colorado Springs,
Deadwood, Denver, Leadville, Marysville, Sacramento, San Francisco, Tombstone, Virginia City)
(1849-1859)

1454 Lestrud, Vernon. "Early Theatrical 'Blue Laws' on
the Pacific Coast. " Rendezvous, 4 (1969), 15-24.
(California, Oregon, Washington) (1850-1899)

1455 Morison, Samuel E. "Commodore Perry's Japan Ex-
pedition Press and Shipboard Theatre. " Proceedings
of the American Antiquarian Society, 77 (April,
1967), 35-43. (1853)

1456 Garner, Madelyn Leora. "The Early Theatre of the
Rocky Mountain West. " M. A. University of Den-
ver, 1935. (Colorado, Idaho, Montana, Utah,
Wyoming) (-1882)

1457 Schwarz, Lyle Allen. "Theatre on the Gold Frontier:
A Cultural Study of Five Northwest Mining Towns,
1860-1870. " Ph. D. Washington State University,
1975. 358 p. [76-04379] (Boise, Helena, Idaho
City, Virginia City, Walla Walla)

1458   Davis, Ronald LeRoy. "A History of Resident Opera
       in the American West. " Ph. D. University of Texas,
       Austin, 1961. 517 p. [61-04686]

1459   _____. A History of Opera in The American West.
       Englewood Cliffs, N. J. : Prentice-Hall, 1965.
       178 p.

1460   _____. "Sopranos and Six-guns: The Frontier Op-
       era House as a Cultural Symbol. " American West,
       7 (November, 1970), 10-17, 63. (1860's)

1461   Van Orman, Richard A. "The Bard in the West. "
       Western Historical Quarterly, 5 (January, 1974),
       29-38. (19th century)

1462   Jordan, Chester I. "A History of Theatre Architecture
       in the Rocky Mountain Region to 1900. " M. A. Uni-
       versity of Wyoming, 1968.

1463   Glyer, Richard Theodore, Jr. "Frank Bacon and His
       Work in the Theatres of the West (1880-1910). "
       M. A. Stanford University, 1941.

1464   Hall, Linda. "Lillie Langtry and the American West. "
       Journal of Popular Culture, 7 (Spring, 1974), 873-
       881. (1880's)

1465   Salsbury, Nate. "The Origin of the Wild West Show. "
       Colorado Magazine, 32 (1955), 205-211.

MISCELLANEOUS

1466 Rosenbach, A. S. W. "The First Theatrical Company in America. " Proceedings of the American Antiquarian Society, New Series, 48 (October, 1938), 300-310. (Lima, Peru) (1599-)

1467 Young, William C. Documents of American Theater History: Vol. 1: Famous American Playhouses, 1716-1899. Chicago: American Library Association, 1973. 316 p.

1468 Bristow, Eugene K. , and William R. Reardon. "Box Office, U. S. A. , 1864-1870: Regional Profiles. " Theatre Survey, 8 (November, 1967), 112-126.

1469 Nolan, Paul T. "Research Projects Waiting: The Forgotten Drama of Provincial America. " Western Speech, 27 (Summer, 1963), 142-150.

1470 _____, ed. Provincial Drama in America, 1870-1916: A Casebook of Primary Materials. Metuchen, N. J. : Scarecrow, 1967.

1471 Morton, Terry Brust. "Town Hall Tonight. " Historic Preservation, 18 (January-February, 1966), 8-19. (Columbus, Georgia; New Harmony, Indiana; Oshkosh, Wisconsin; Peninsula, Ohio)

1472 Chesley, Gene A. "Encore for 19th-century American Theaters. " Historic Preservation, 25 (October-December, 1973), 20-25. (California, Colorado, Connecticut, Iowa)

BIBLIOGRAPHIES

1473   "The Theatre in Missouri. " Missouri Historical Review, 28 (October, 1933), 53.

1474   Hamar, Clifford E. "American Theatre History: A Geographical Index. " Educational Theatre Journal, 1 (December, 1949), 164-194.

1475   Hewitt, Barnard. "American Theatre and Drama in the XVIII Century: A Bibliographical Essay. " Theatre Research, 1 (June, 1958), 21-25.

1476   Carson, William G. B. "The Theatre of the American Frontier: A Bibliographical Essay. " Theatre Research, 1 (1958), 14-23.

1477   Brockett, Oscar G. "The Theatre of the Southern United States from the Beginnings through 1865: A Bibliographical Essay. " Theatre Research, 2 (1960), 163-174.

1478   Marshall, Thomas F. "Beyond New York: A Bibliography of the 19th Century American Stage from the Atlantic to the Mississippi. " Theatre Research, 3 (1961), 208-217.

1479   Cole, Wendell. "Early Theatre in America West of the Rockies: A Bibliographical Essay. " Theatre Research, 4 (1962), 36-45.

1480   Watson, Charles S. "Eighteenth and Nineteenth Century Drama. " A Bibliographical Guide to the Study of Southern Literature. Ed. Louis D. Rubin, Jr. Baton Rouge: Louisiana State University Press, 1969. pp. 92-99.

1481   Shaver, Claude L.; David Ritchey, and Gresdna Doty. "Southern Theatre History: A Bibliography of Theses and Dissertations. " Southern Speech Communication Journal, 42 (Summer, 1977), 362-373.

FOREIGN LANGUAGE THEATRE INDEX

Chinese 122

Czech 364

French 429, 430, 431, 435, 436, 457, 538, 1044, 1045,
1078, 1079, 1147

German 36, 86, 93, 101, 291, 292, 366, 367, 369, 415,
474, 475, 543, 546, 666, 699, 705, 706, 707, 708, 709,
755, 774, 775, 776, 788, 894, 939, 940, 948, 1050, 1051,
1052, 1053, 1055, 1056, 1057, 1082, 1159, 1378, 1379,
1380, 1381, 1382, 1383, 1448

Norwegian 301

Spanish 21, 846, 847, 848, 849, 850, 851, 852, 853, 854,
855, 856, 857, 858, 859, 1041, 1234

Swedish 306, 307, 308

PERSONS AS SUBJECT INDEX

171

AUTHOR INDEX

Watson, Charles Sullivan
1148, 1154, 1155, 1165,
1344, 1480
Watson, Margaret G. 819,
829
Webb, Dorothy Louise Beck
1077
Webster, Mary Viola 65
Wegelin, Oscar 381
Weinfeld, Samuel L. 354
Weisert, John Jacob 401,
409, 410, 411, 412, 413,
414, 415, 416, 421
Welsh, Willard 1430
Wente, William Charles 52
West, William Francis, Jr.
790
West, William Russell 227
Westcott, Thompson 1095
Westhafer, Steven James
1202
Wetmore, Thomas H., Jr.
910
White, Irle E. 988
White, Matthew, Jr. 1275
Whitehead, Marjorie 75
Whiting, Frank M. 697,
698
Whitney, Horace G. 1280
Widem, Allen M. 187
Wiedenthal, Maurice 961
Wiedersheim, William A.,
II 1090
Wilkinson, Alfred Oliver
758
Wilkinson, Colleen Mae 762
Willard, George Owen 1117
Willis, Eola 1127
Wills, J. Robert 954
Willson, Clair Eugene 17,
18, 19
Willson, Loretta Lyle 380
Wilmeth, Don B. 324, 1413
Wilson, Arthur Herman
1080, 1081
Wilson, Bertha Amelia 978
Wilson, Jack A. 658

Wilson, Robert 277
Wilson, Willard 264
Wilson, William F. 259
Wilt, James Napier 289, 301
Wingate, Charles Edgar Lewis
615
Wingerter, Charles A. 1367
Wixander, Laurence E. 644
Wolcott, John Rutherford
1047, 1048, 1074
Wolf, Edwin, II 1409
Wolfert, Wayne Richard 1368
Wood, Ralph Charles 939,
940, 948
Woodruff, Boykin Maxwell, Jr.
7
Woodruff, John Rowland 549,
597
Woods, Alan Lambert 44, 45
Woods, Donald Z. 688, 689
Woodward, Dorothy 844
Wooten, Denham Lee 24, 34
Worner, William Frederic
1008, 1010, 1011, 1012,
1014
Wright, Harriette E. 428
Wright, James W. 305
Wyatt, Edward A., IV 1301
Wyman, Henry A. 614

Yaari, Moshe 42
Yalof, Helen Roberta 1035
Yeaton, Kelly 1415
Yeomans, Gordon Allen 1425
Yocum, Jack Harlan 1223
Yonick, Cora Jane 332
Young, James Harvey 607
Young, John P. 1189
Young, William C. 1467
Youngerman, Henry Clayman
1370, 1371

Zalusky, Joseph 691
Zern, Frank W. 164
Zucker, Adolf E. 543